THE LUCKY AUDIOPHILE
ANECDOTES FROM HIGH-END AUDIO

My Charmed Journey
Through Music and Stereo Equipment

By Michael Kuller
Former Reviewer for *The Absolute Sound*

D1713586

The Lucky Audiophile: Anecdotes from High-End Audio by Michael Kuller

Copyright © 2022 by Michael Kuller

Published by
Michael Kuller
1985 Cactus Ct. #1
Walnut Creek, CA 94595
Mkuller1@gmail.com

To order, visit www.amazon.com

ISBN. 979-8-3751-3740-7

Since I've written all of this from memory, with a little help from Google, please forgive me if I get dates or other details wrong. It surprises me how vivid and detailed some of these memories are though.

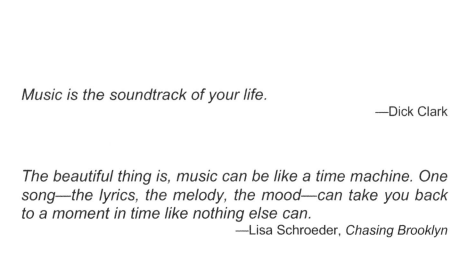

Music is the soundtrack of your life.

—Dick Clark

The beautiful thing is, music can be like a time machine. One song—the lyrics, the melody, the mood—can take you back to a moment in time like nothing else can.

—Lisa Schroeder, *Chasing Brooklyn*

Table of Contents

Preface

In Malcolm Gladwell's popular 2008 book, *Outliers, The Stories of Success*, outliers are those given the ability to succeed by being in the right place at the right time. To realize that ability, they have worked very hard at something they loved.

Of course, success is dependent on many personal traits, like intelligence, talent and hard work. But the things he argues that can make as much difference are the year you were born and finding a niche you are passionate enough about that you are willing to put in hard work to master it.

Gladwell explains how 1953–1956 were the ideal years in which to have been born for the computer revolution that took off in the mid-1970s. As it turns out, Bill Gates, Paul Allen and Steve Ballmer (all of Microsoft fame), as well as Steve Jobs (Apple) and Eric Schmidt (Google), were all born between 1953 and 1956. Coincidence? Hardly, according to Gladwell.

Steve Jobs grew up in Mountain View, CA near Silicon Valley and Hewlett-Packard. His neighborhood was full of HP engineers who he used to chat with and get computer parts from. He attended evening talks given by the HP scientists. Not only did he call HP cofounder, Bill Hewlett, to request some parts, but he even managed to wrangle a summer job from Hewlett assembling computers. He was so fascinated with them, he tried to design his own computer.

In the eighth grade, Bill Gates went to one of the first high schools in the country to have computer club, when most universities didn't have computers. Then he lucked into gaining nearly unlimited use of the computers at the University of Washington. By the time he was 20 years old, he had put in over 10,000 hours of computer programming.

That is the 10,000-hour rule identified by neurologist Daniel Levitin (who also wrote, *This is Your Brain on Music*). It's the amount of time you must invest in anything to gain real expertise in that field. As with Gates and Jobs, the superstars of anything, Gladwell and Levitin argue, get good by outworking everyone else, and not just by a small margin. Passable pianists might practice an hour or two a day growing up, which is clearly a lot more than most people who dabble at the keyboard practice. But professional pianists—those who appear onstage at Carnegie Hall—start practicing five or six hours a day in their teenage years. They're *that good* because they practice *that much.*

The Beatles are another example. From 1960 through 1962 they made 5 trips to Hamburg to play in the strip clubs and brothels there because it was steady work that paid well. They performed 8 to 12 hours a night seven days a week for 270 nights over that 2.5 years. By the time they became successful in 1964, they had played together live more than 1,200 times! That's easily 10,000 hours learning to play an incredible number of different songs together as a group. Many artists never play that much in an entire career.

Gladwell says, "Hard work is a prison sentence only if it does not have meaning" and highlights some of the qualities of work that infuse it with meaning. If it isn't meaningful to you, it's a safe bet you won't want to put in the time needed to master it. If the work is meaningful, those 10,000 hours may just fly by. *Besides these famous people Gladwell calls outliers, he discusses many more in his book who are just ordinary people.*

I feel I have had the good fortune of experiencing this effect first hand. Because of when I was born and the opportunities I was presented in pursuing the things that I was passionate about, I was very fortunate to have traveled the charmed path through music and audio I recount here. I call it charmed and fortunate because I was very lucky in many ways.

Chapter One
The Early Years

My journey of good fortune began with my birth into a stable, happy, middle-class family in Monterey, CA, at the beginning of the postwar boom in 1947. My mother was 20 when I was born. I don't think much music played in the house where she grew up in, so she liked the newer rock and roll music. As long as I can remember, I've always loved this music. When I was two years old, we moved to Texas. As a kid growing up in New Braunfels, near San Antonio, the only music being played in my home was my mother's AM radio over the kitchen sink in the 1950s, with Chuck Berry, Elvis, the Coasters, Little Richard and all the other early rock and rollers.

In the third through the sixth grade summers, I would ride my bicycle down to the local Landa Park swimming pool (the largest freshwater pool in Texas—way before the Schlitterbahn). I would hang out there for five or six hours a day and hear the jukebox playing constantly: songs like "Willie and the Hand Jive" and "CC Rider," artists like Jerry Lee Lewis, Buddy Holly, Fats Domino, the Diamonds, the Olympics and Jan and Arnie (who became Jan and Dean).

When I was in fifth grade, about five or six of us would stay in the classroom at lunch and listen to 45 RPM records people brought in. Larry Williams' "Short Fat Fanny" and "At the Hop" were a couple of my favorites.

That year for XMas my parents bought me a 45 RPM record player, a box with the tall, fat spindle on it. My uncle, a couple of years younger than my mother, gave me five 45 RPM records, some Elvis and a Conway Twitty. I remember the first few records I bought were Link Wray's "Rumble," "I've Had It" by the Bell Notes and the "Book of Love" by the Monotones. My best friend, Jerry, had a brother a couple of years older, who swore the words in "Searchin'," by the Coasters, where the singer sings falsetto, were, "like f**kin' brother." It was incredible to hear that in a popular song on the radio. The words are really "like Bulldog Drummond," but we didn't recognize the name and it was difficult to understand on the AM radios of the day.

Occasionally, I'd watch American Bandstand and really liked to see them do the Stroll. It was a dance even I could do. There was some great Doo-Wop during this period, too— "Blue Moon," "I Only Have Eyes For You," "Get a Job" and many others. I watched Ozzie and Harriet each week, mainly to see Ricky Nelson sing at the end.

In 1958, he hit #1 with "Poor Little Fool" and it was on the US pop charts for 15 weeks.

In the sixth grade, I recall my teacher, Mrs. Christianson, telling us that she and her husband bought a stereo, the first one I had heard of. Stereos then were big consoles with a record changer under the top and built-in speakers on each side.

Buddy Holly, Ritchie Valens and the Big Bopper died that year in a plane crash. I remember where I was when I heard about it, walking on the school breezeway after lunch—just like people recall where they were when hearing about the Kennedy assassination.

Around that time, I decided I wanted to learn to play the guitar. I had saved my allowance and we bought a cheap one through the Sears catalog, where we bought most of our things. My mother hooked me up with an older woman down the street who played the piano to give me lessons. After several sessions of trying to play "She'll Be Coming Around the Mountain" and "My Darling Clementine," I gave it up. It was too slow and too boring.[1]

I went to summer camp in Kerrville during a couple of summers at 12 and 13 years of age. The second summer, I met a

---

[1] Much later, when my daughter took guitar lessons in middle school, she learned from the Tom Petty songbook.

Michael Kuller

kid named Mike Hodges who could play the piano. He taught me a cool boogie-woogie riff while everyone else seemed to be playing "Heart and Soul" on the cafeteria piano.

Besides music, I had a couple of other hobbies when I was 13 and 14. I was building model cars[2] and listening to ham radio. The father of a couple of good friends was a ham radio operator and they were both studying to get their ham licenses. I was going to take the test with them but decided I didn't want to learn the morse code so I just stuck with listening to the ham operators' chatter around the country. Here, I began honing my listening skills.

In the summer of 1963, for my junior year in high school, we moved to Roswell, New Mexico. Early on, I wrecked my Vespa (that I had used for my morning paper route in Texas) one

---

[2] My customized 1940 Ford won the first prize trophy in the Model Car Division of the 1961 Dallas Rod and Custom Show.

evening and broke my kneecap.[3] Two other things that stand out from that year were the "dirty lyrics" of "Louie, Louie" being passed around class and President Kennedy's assassination.

In the summer of 1964 before our senior year in high school, I saw my first component stereo. One of my best friends, Ritchie, received it for his birthday. He now had a Fisher receiver, Scott speakers and a Garrard record changer in his bedroom. We used to sit on his bed and listen to the Rolling Stones' *12 X 5* album. Whenever I hear the song, "2120 South Michigan Avenue," I'm taken back there.

In October of 1964, we learned about the first live concert to be simulcast to movie theaters all across the country, called the T.A.M.I. Show. We went to the local drive-in the evening of the telecast to watch it, sitting on the hood of my 1957 Ford. It featured all of the popular artists of the day with Shindig-like dancers on scaffolds behind many of them: Jan and Dean, the Beach Boys, Gerry and the Pacemakers, Marvin Gaye, the Supremes, Smokey Robinson, Lesley Gore, an amazing long set by James Brown that blew everybody away, and then the headliners, The Rolling Stones, on their first American tour.[4] What a show! I still love watching the DVD today.

My sister, two years younger, had a record player and bought Beatles and Beach Boys records that were always playing in our house. I had my car and a portable transistor radio that I had to rely on to hear the latest music. I still recall the thrill of hearing "I Want to Hold Your Hand" by that English group with the strange haircuts, as they called them. We went to see the local band, The Mystics, whenever they played teen dances.

---

[3] I hit a parked pick-up truck going about 30mph, went over the handlebars hitting my knee and landed on a couch in the back of the truck. Wasn't that lucky?

[4] When the VHS recording of the TAMI Show was made, they cut out about half of James Brown's performance because he had upstaged the headlining Rolling Stones. At the end, they tacked on another small concert from 1966 called the TNT Show with a number of performers who mostly weren't in the TAMI Show, like Ray Charles, Bo Diddley and Ike and Tina Turner. When they made the DVD of the TAMI Show they restored James Brown's performance and eliminated the TNT footage.

Michael Kuller

Their guitar player was excellent and could do the double-picking of "Miserlou," my favorite song at the time. I knew the bass player, Gilbert, and the drummer, Logan, who excelled on "Wipe Out." They were both in my year in high school.

I soon became aware of a terrific LP, called *Surfin' with the Astronauts,* recorded live in 1963 at Tulagi's Club in Boulder, CO. A lot of the high school kids in Roswell wanted to be surf-ers.[5] A couple even had woodies (one was a Morris Minor). One rich blond girl spent a couple of weeks during the summer in LA with her family on vacation. When she came back, she told everyone she had dated Brian Wilson.

My senior year of high school was much like "American Graffiti." There was a drive-in burger place on one end of town where everyone hung out, cruising back and forth down Main Street and occasionally choosing off to drag race outside of town. There was some great music on the radio that year—"Satisfaction," "Pretty Woman," "I Can't Help Myself," "Girl from Ipanema," "Help Me Rhonda," "My Girl" and "The House of the Rising Sun." That year, there was a concert by the Sir Douglas Quintet ("She's About a Mover") announced at the local armory. I kicked myself for not getting tickets until I read afterward that it was a fake cover band and people were looking for the promoter to get their money back. The next concert at the armory was my first—by the Pyramids, a surf band with their hit, "Penetration."

Ritchie spent some time that summer after we graduated high school working in New Orleans. When he came back, he played a record for me that he said was getting a lot of air play there, Bob Dylan's "Like a Rolling Stone." I thought it was pretty interesting and had never heard it in Roswell. We decided to take it to the local radio station and ask them to play it. We went into the radio station and told the DJ we had a record we wanted him to play. He said, "If it's by Bob Dylan, you can forget it. I'm not playing it." So we left. In a month or so, they were playing it because it had gotten so popular.

---

[5] No one talked about or seemed to be aware of the 1947 UFO/alien incident until the 50th anniversary when the Roswell UFO Museum opened.

Chapter Two
The Middle Years

In the fall of 1965, the next phase of my journey of fortune began as I started college at Eastern New Mexico University (ENMU) in Portales. It was a small school with around 3,000 students. During the first couple of weeks at school, I ran into Mike Hodges, the piano player from summer camp in Texas. He told me he had played piano on the hit song, "Last Kiss" by J. Frank Wilson and the Cavaliers.[6] "Where, oh where can my baby be ...." Wow!

In my first semester, ENMU had three fraternities, and I pledged Pi Kappa Alpha. Before finals that fall, we did a long-weekend pledge sneak to visit a chapter at another school. We kidnapped the most popular active member, Sid, who was smart and very funny and took him with us. We ended up at the Pi Kappa Alpha house at the University of Colorado in Boulder. It was by far the coolest college campus I had ever seen; 20,000 students nestled at the base of the mountains. The fraternity invited us to a party they were throwing that Friday afternoon with a sorority and kegs. I checked the out-of-state tuition; it was more than we could afford.

That fall I saw a concert on campus in the ENMU gym—We Five and the Righteous Brothers. We used to watch "Where the Action Is" with Paul Revere and the Raiders on TV in the afternoons; it came on after "Batman." At night, we were able to listen to radio station KOMA from Oklahoma City, which had a pretty wide broadcast area, and radio station XERB across the border in Mexico, where the original Wolfman Jack broadcast with "50,000 watts of power." The other music I recall from that year was "Mr. Tambourine Man" by the Byrds and Barry McGuire's "Eve of Destruction."

I dropped a class in the spring semester of 1966, which put me below the 16 units needed for a draft deferment, and got a draft notice for the Vietnam War. After my physical, where they became aware of the wire holding my kneecap together,

---

[6] The song was covered in 2000 by Pearl Jam.

I was rated 1Y, to be called up only in case of a national emergency. My knee hasn't bothered me all these years so I guess that was a pretty lucky crash after all.

Zenith Stereo

In 1966, after a year in college, I was in San Bernardino, CA for the summer. My mother called and told me my father got a new job; my family was moving to—of all places—Boulder, CO. Are you kidding me? How lucky can I get?

I had to wait for my parents to live a year in Colorado to gain residency so I could go to the University of Colorado in Boulder. So, with no draft worries, I stayed out of school for the year. I bought a green Zenith record player with detachable speakers while living in an apartment. My roommate (who had joined the Navy Reserve to avoid the draft) and I both worked at Chevron gas stations for the year, with the white uniforms, black bow ties, ice cream hats, full service and $0.39/gallon gasoline. It seems like the Beatles and the Mamas and Papas came out with new records every couple of months. I recall seeing the Beatles' new album *Yesterday and Today* with them in white butcher coats and cut up baby dolls on display across the window of a store, but I didn't buy it that day. I'm not sure what put me off, but the cover was a little disturbing and was a big departure from their previous cover on *Rubber Soul.* A few days later when I came back to get the album, the cover had changed. The original cover is now worth a lot of money.

The Monkees were big, as was Junior Walker and Paul Revere and the Raiders. The Beach Boys came out with their masterpiece, "Good Vibrations" and the Beatles with "Penny Lane" and "Strawberry Fields" that year.

A couple of friends and I drove down to Crescent Bay in Laguna Beach to body surf one day and one of them brought a battery-powered record player. We had *The Rolling Stones Now* album and listened to it a few times in the back of my small station wagon. I really liked their song, "Mona," but didn't know it was a cover of a Bo Diddley song at the time. During the early summer of 1967, the Doors' "Light My Fire" seemed to play almost constantly on the LA radio stations.

When I saw Tarantino's excellent 2019 film, "Once Upon a Time in Hollywood," it took me right back to that time in Southern California. I remember listening to the Real Don Steele on KHJ radio, who Tarantino showcases, but my favorite was B. Mitchell Reed—BMR on KFWB.

In the fall of 1967, I took the Zenith with me back to school at the Colorado University, was invited to join Pi Kappa Alpha and used it in my fraternity house room for the next two years. This was the beginning of the classic rock explosion, and exciting new music was everywhere. 3.2 beer was legal in Colorado for 18 year olds, so the two places on the Hill, Tulagi's Club and The Sink, sold more Coors than anywhere else in the country. The house band at Tulagi's seemed to play

Michael Kuller

"Gimme Some Lovin'" and "Under My Thumb" every night for dancing. Thursdays was nickel beer and dollar pitcher night.

Hendrix's first album, *Are You Experienced* had come out, Cream's "Sunshine of Your Love" played constantly on the Sink's jukebox, as did the Box Tops' "The Letter" on the radio. In the fraternity house and at house parties, it seemed like Motown and R & B were always playing—the Temptations, Marvin Gaye, Aretha, The Four Tops, Wilson Picket and the Supremes.

I bought my first blues record, from Muddy Waters, but it wasn't *Folk Singer.* It was *Electric Mud,* which is a few of his standard songs backed by a psychedelic rock band. It also has a great picture on the album cover of him in a long white robe with a priceless look on his face. Blues purists hate this album, but I think it's kind of fun and it did introduce me to Muddy Waters.

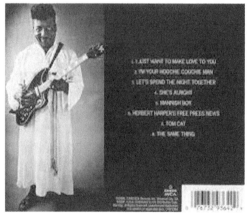

Electric Mud

While living at the fraternity house, I noticed that the mailman would sometimes leave packs of records from the Columbia Record Club addressed to strange names. They advertised everywhere that you could get 12 albums for $1 as long as you agreed to buy one a month at the regular price for the next year. The strange names were used by my fraternity brothers to get free records. If you didn't pay, Columbia would send collection letters but nothing more. Wow, free music. So I figured I would get in on it. After picking the first six or so records, it became difficult to find more on their list that I didn't already have and wanted. So I got exposed to a lot of new music through the record club ordering 12 at a time a few times over the two years I was there. They included The Electric Flag, Jobim's *Wave,* Friends of Distinction, Hugh Masekela, and the 5th Dimension.

My years in the fraternity house presaged *Animal House*. We actually had a toga party, and black bands from Denver would come play at our parties. A buddy and I even took dates to Denver to see one of those bands play at a small club and we were the only white people there. Unlike in *Animal House,* everyone was very nice to us and our dates.

During the summer of 1968, I was living in Boulder and ran into Sid, the fraternity member from ENMU we had taken with us on our pledge sneak. He was living in an apartment in Broomfield, between Boulder and Denver. I hung out a little with him that summer and recall going over to his place and him telling me, "I have a record I want you to hear." He dropped the album down on his Benjamin-Miracord turntable and handed me the album cover. It was *Nico and the Velvet Underground,* with the Andy Warhol designed and signed cover featuring a peelable yellow banana on it. The singer was Lou Reed who I would recognize later when he came out with his solo stuff. The music was pretty raw but engaging and not easy to forget.

Michael Kuller

914 Broadway

1967/1968—Pi Kappa Alphas—I'm in the upper left window holding the guy hanging out.

At the end of the 1968–69 school year, the fraternity folded. When I started, there were 21 fraternities at CU and ours was the only house that was actually on campus property, next to Regents Hall. Our pledges and the younger guys no longer wanted to live in the frat house and drink beer. They preferred to have their own apartments so they could smoke pot and have girls over, not that there's anything wrong with that. A number of other fraternities closed that same year as the culture shifted with the Vietnam War protests, drugs and hippies. Without enough people living in the house to pay the mortgage, the national fraternity took it back and sold it to the University. At first it housed Campus Security and then became the President of CU's residence. Again, timing is everything. I really enjoyed the fraternity for those two years but was happy to move on.

I didn't have much money since I was putting myself through school waiting tables and then bartending, but I always made sure I had enough for records and concert tickets. I saw some great concerts during my college years—See Appendix I: Concerts

- The Doors played on New Year's Eve in 1967 at The Family Dog in Denver to a fairly small audience. There was a light show and it was terrific seeing the band live since I had heard their music on the radio and their first album played over and over on my Zenith record player.

- Jimi Hendrix was incredible at the small Regis College Field House in Denver on his first tour in the spring of 1968. He played his guitar behind his back and with his teeth. At the end, he set it on fire.

Jimi Hendrix

- In the summer of 1968, a buddy and I walked into some teen fair going on in a large building in downtown Denver. In the expansive entry, there were Felix Cavaliere and the Young Rascals playing. They had a couple of hits, but I always thought they were underrated: They had so many more good songs on their albums.

- Mountain came to the CU campus the day after playing in Denver two years in a row and put on a free concert on a practice field. One year, they brought Blues Image as their opening act. I recall the first time I heard their song, "Mississippi Queen," on the radio. I went out the next day and bought their album. Seeing Leslie West singing and playing slide guitar with Felix Pappalardi on bass egging him on with Corky Lang playing drums and throwing drum sticks up into the air all up very close was a great experience.

Mountain

- I saw the Four Tops in Miami on Spring break in 1968. Along with the Temptations, they were my favorite Motown group and put on a great show with all their great dancing moves and songs.

- The Rolling Stones played in 1969 at the Colorado State Gym in Ft. Collins. It became their *Get Your Ya Yas Out* album and the tour that ended with the Altamont disaster. It was one of the best concerts I've ever seen. Their *Let It Bleed* album had just come out; they played "Midnight Rambler" and ended the concert with "Street Fighting Man." The opening acts were David Essex ("Rock On") and B. B. King.

- Janis Joplin/Big Brother and Steve Miller played on a round rotating stage in Denver. I liked Janis Joplin's *Cheap Thrills* album, but was probably more impressed with R. Crumb's artwork on the album cover. Steve Miller's earlier work was much better than his pop-synthesizer music later in the 1970s. I don't know why the rotating stage was ever a thing because no one had good seats.

- Santana and Crosby, Stills and Nash played Denver in 1969, fresh on their first tour from Woodstock. Santana's first two albums are my favorites of theirs because they capture the Afro-Cuban percussion and Hammond B3 vibe better than of any of their later releases. Guitarist Neal Schon and B3 keyboardist Greg Rollie left the band in 1973 to found the group Journey.

  Crosby, Stills and Nash continued the vocal harmonies from the Beach Boys and the Mamas and Papas. David Crosby was from the Byrds and was one of the key players in the Laurel Canyon music scene, dating the women and introducing the musicians to each other, helping to form the shifting music groups. For example, after dating Joni Mitchell, he introduced her to Graham Nash from the Hollies, who she lived with in "Our House." Stephen Stills was a genius guitarist, multi-instrument musician and songwriter from Buffalo Springfield. He had played with Al Cooper, in place of Michael Bloomfield, on half of the *Super Session* album. Crosby introduced them to the Canadian musician, Neil Young, who joined them on and off. The group made some of the most memorable light rock music of the era.

- I missed one concert that some of the guys in my fraternity got tickets to see. It was Cream playing at the Denver Arena. I'm not sure why I missed it since I really liked their *Disraeli Gears* and *Wheels of Fire* albums.

About that time, in 1969, after Woodstock happened, I noticed a new magazine about rock music and counterculture called *The Rolling Stone*, and subscribed to it.

Walking across the CU campus one day, I ran into Logan, the drummer for the Mystics, who had been in my 11th grade English class in Roswell. No, he didn't play drums on "In-A-Gadda-Da-Vida" or anything like that, but it was quite a surprise to see him going to school there.

KLH Model 11 Compact Stereo

In 1970, we were living in a rental house and I bought a KLH Compact system at the Jones Drug and Camera on the Hill. KLH had just been sold to the Singer Company and the store had both an older KLH Compact and a newer one from Singer. I brought along the new Rolling Stones album, *Sticky Fingers* and used the song, "Brown Sugar" to compare them. Bobby

Keys' saxophone sounded better to me on the new model, so I bought it.

Sticky Fingers zipper cover
designed by Andy Warhol

View from beside our
rental house in Boulder

The rental house was just at the edge of town to the south, past the Table Mesa shopping center. Our landlords managed the Caribou Guest Ranch north of town, up Boulder Canyon on the way to Nederland. We went up there once to pay our rent and check the place out. There was a big barn for the horses, a main guest house and a number of smaller cottages. It looked like a fun place for a cowboy-type dude ranch vacation.

Caribou Ranch

After living in that house for about a year, one evening we got a call from our landlords telling us the guest ranch had been sold and they needed to move back into our house. They gave us our 30 days' notice. It turns out Caribou Ranch had been sold to Bob Guercio, the producer of the group Chicago, who wanted to turn it into a state-of-the-art recording studio. A fraternity friend of mine working in his father's real estate office at the time told me this was the biggest real estate deal Boulder had seen in a long time. The agent who made the sale had been in the popular Catacombs Bar in the basement of the Boulderado Hotel the night the deal closed buying drinks for everyone there. Since we had just been kicked out of our house, I've always thought we should have been invited.

"In Guercio's barn turned studio, Joe Walsh recorded the first album that came out of Caribou Ranch, the eponymous 1972 Barnstorm. The barn conversion was not yet complete, but the dirt floors were only a tribute to the remote, creative ambiance. "Rocky Mountain Way" was the first hit recorded at Caribou, and soon after word got out that Mr. Guercio had created a state of the art recording studio far away from big city distractions and frenzied scenes.

As the first destination recording studio, music history was made by illustrious artists and groups such as Elton John, Stephen Stills, Billy Joel, Chicago, Earth, Wind & Fire, The

Beach Boys, Michael Jackson, Johnny Cash, Rod Stewart, Frank Zappa, Jerry Lee Lewis, Stevie Nicks, Tom Petty, U2 and many more. Wildly popular songs from the 1970s and 80s were written and recorded on the ranch that include chart topping hits such as Earth, Wind & Fire's "Shining Star," Chicago's "If You Leave Me Now," and Elton John's "Philadelphia Freedom.""

From the *Mountain Music, Arts and Culture Monthly,* January 9, 2015

Chicago at Caribou
From the Caribou Ranch Colorado Mus
Experien

Michael Murphy ("Wildfire") in the Studio
Note the blue oxygen tank – altitude of 8,€
From the Caribou Ranch Recording Studio Faceboc

- The Who's *Who's Next* Denver concert in 1971 was fantastic and one of my favorite albums. They are one of the best live rock bands. Sadly, rock's greatest drummer, Keith Moon, died in 1978.

- Rod Stewart and the Faces' *Every Picture Tells a Story* concert tour came to Denver. He had been a soccer player and was very athletic running around on the stage holding the microphone stand with a long scarf around his neck. I've always admired Ian McLagan's keyboard playing. They closed with "I Know I'm Losing You" from that album, which has one of my favorite drum solos.

- In 1970 Joe Walsh and the James Gang released *The James Gang Rides Again,* one of my favorites. It was guitar-oriented rock but with a few flourishes like "The Bomber Medley," which includes parts of "Bolero" and "Cast Your Fate to the Wind," and his classical music inspired "The Ashes, the Rain and I". I saw James Gang in Denver two years in a row.

- I even saw Black Sabbath and John Kay of Steppenwolf. I wasn't really a fan of either band, but there were six of us going so I went along. It didn't change my feelings about either group.

- I went to an Elton John concert at the Denver Arena on his *Tumbleweed Connections* Tour where he wore shorts and had only Nigel Olsson on drums and Dee Murray on bass. He ended the concert with the song, "Burn Down the Mission" and he was all over the piano. It was a very exciting concert. This was before he went glam and I knew he'd be a big star.

Red Rocks, outside of Denver, is an amazing concert venue where I saw Mountain again, 10 Years After (with great guitarist Alvin Lee), Vanilla Fudge ("You Keep Me Hanging On"), Hugh Masekela ("Grazing in the Grass") and Woody Herman.

Red Rocks

At the CU fieldhouse I saw Fleetwood Mac (after Peter Green, but before Buckingham/Nicks), Savoy Brown (*Street Corner Talking*), Zephyr (*Sunset Ride*) and West, Bruce and Laing (not as good without Felix Pappalardi).

I had tickets to see Traffic at the Denver Arena but on the way my girlfriend said she wasn't feeling good so we decided to skip the concert and go home. I stopped by the Arena and sold my tickets to a couple of guys outside for face value—$15 ea. I wish I could have seen that one.[7]

---

[7] Fortunately, I did get to see Steve Winwood and Jim Capaldi on their Traffic Reunion Tour in 1994, sadly without Dave Mason and Chris Wood.

Michael Kuller

After graduating and working as a pharmacist at a hospital in Denver in 1972, a female pharmacist colleague told me her husband sold stereo equipment. She brought me one of her husband's *Stereo Review* magazines. In it, Julian Hirsch reviewed the Infinity 2000a speaker (with electrostatic tweeters) giving it an A− grade. This was my first time seeing *Stereo Review,* and here Julian Hirsch was actually giving letter grades. Later, he would be ridiculed by audiophiles for his wishy-washy conclusions about products based solely on their measurements.

Infinity 2000a speakers

ım cover picture from Caribou Ranch

ıe Walsh and Barnstorm

That year, Joe Walsh was living in the mountains above Boulder recording his *Barnstorm* album at Caribou Ranch. He and the band came down to the small Tulagi's Club on the Hill and performed a concert. I can still hear Joe Vitale hit the big kettle drums and hanging Chinese gong in "Mother Says." It was a terrific concert and is one of my favorite Joe Walsh albums. Do you know how Joe Walsh and Ringo are related?[8]

The next year, 1973, I moved to Long Beach, CA with everything I owned in a VW van and then bought my first real stereo at Pacific Stereo, the only stereo store I was aware of. My Asian pharmacist colleagues from USC were all driving used Porsches they bought after graduating, but I bought myself a stereo first. When I went into Pacific Stereo, I picked out the Infinity 2000axt speakers (with the Walsh ice-cream-cone tweeter) among a lineup of about a dozen speakers. After reading the *Stereo Review* article lauding the earlier Infinity speaker, I was predisposed to thinking it sounded good, although in the demo room, among a lineup of different speakers, it sounded a little bright with Bonnie Raitt's voice. I bought them anyway. I added a Kenwood Quadraphonic receiver and a dual record changer and later on picked up some smaller KLH speakers on sale for their rear channels.[9] I was ready to rock.

Infinity 2000axt speakers

I stuck the Infinity speakers in the corners of the living room of our rented duplex near the beach. It seems like we had music playing pretty much all the time.

Classic rock continued to grow through the 1970s and living in Southern California I was fortunate to be exposed to many of the Topanga/Laurel Canyon LA music scene resident

---

[8] In 2008 Joe Walsh married Marjorie Bach, the sister of Ringo's wife, Barbara Bach. They are brothers-in-law.

[9] Later, Harry Pearson of *The Absolute Sound* magazine would joke that I had better speakers in the rear than in the front.

Michael Kuller

musicians of the era. I remember we went to Doug Weston's Troubadour Club once where they all played, but I don't recall who we saw there. We went to concerts at the Santa Monica Civic and then the Universal Amphitheater all summers long. We saw Jackson Browne, Linda Ronstadt, Bonnie Raitt, the Eagles, Seals and Croft, Joni Mitchell, Loggins and Messina, Fleetwood Mac and Dave Mason. A new comedian, Steve Martin, opened for a Linda Ronstadt concert with a white suit and an arrow through his head. Funny guy.

A few of the other new artist's albums I recall being released during this time were Boston, Foreigner, Kansas, Bad Company and Peter Frampton's live album.

We saw Joan Baez at the Hollywood Bowl. I remember her singing "Amazing Grace" acapella, with the purity of her voice projecting out over the absolute silence of the audience.

We saw Led Zeppelin at the Long Beach Arena and when we arrived, we found our seats happened to be behind the stage and the band. We were up fairly close, but after a few songs with John Bonham's drums echoing back to us and obscuring much of the music, we moved to the side and sat in an aisle. No one bothered us there. Powerful concert.

Linda Ronstadt

I remember going to see a Linda Ronstadt concert at Universal. J.D. Souther came out and sang "Prisoner in Disguise" (which he wrote) with her. When she sang "Heart Like a Wheel" a violinist appeared above her from the darkness off to the right. It was a terrific concert. They announced that since the previous night's concerts had been rained out, they had tickets for the rescheduled concerts available for the next couple of nights. So I bought a couple of tickets and went back to see her again. What an amazing voice she had.

Around 1977, I decided I was ready for some new speakers and shopped all around small stores in Long Beach and Orange County. I heard about a half dozen speakers in different stores, but none of them thrilled me. At the time, it seems, everyone was using "Time" from Pink Floyd's *Dark Side of the Moon* to demo equipment and one dealer even had a light show behind the speakers. Then I walked into a Federated chain stereo store in Huntington Beach, with the floor stacked with equipment boxes, to hear the Ohm Fs (which used the Walsh driver inverted as a full range speaker). Someone had told me they were pretty good speakers.

Ohm F Speakers

I was led into the "expensive-speaker room" behind a locked sliding glass door. I listened to the Ohms, which had a lot of bass but didn't seem to be anything special. As we were getting ready to leave, the salesman turned back on some Latin percussion music playing through a pair of Dahlquist DQ-10s on the side of the room. I stopped in my tracks and turned to listen as lifelike sounding instruments came from between, in back of and all around the speakers. Wow, they really knocked my socks off. I decided I had to have them, and my high-end audio journey really began.

Michael Kuller

Dahlquist DQ-10s with Subwoofer

Dahlquist DQ-10 with the front grille removed

At that time I was reading *Audio* magazine and noticed an ad in the back for a new audio review publication called *The Audio Critic*. I subscribed and with my check, sent a letter suggesting they review the DQ-10s with their new subwoofers. They printed my letter in their first issue and coincidentally, the Dahlquists with its subs was their first reference system.

Peter Aczel

The Dahlquists needed a lot of powe
said he preferred the Quatre Gain Cell amps with the DQ-10s,
over than the highly regarded Ampzilla, both rated 200w/ch @
8 ohms. That's when I noticed in the lively *LA Times* audio
classifieds[10] that Quatre was made in the San Fernando Valley and they were having a sale. So I drove up and bought two
($350 ea) to bi-amp the DQ-10s and two subs.

I then discovered a different type of audio store in Huntington
Beach, not far down Harbor Blvd. from the Federated Store,
called Havens and Hardesty. It was a few open rooms with
speakers and systems on display, but without Federated's
stacked boxes on the floor. There were no speakers lined up
like Pacific Stereo or other stereo stores I had been in. They
were dealers for brands I'd never heard of, like Dunlap Clark,
Bowers & Wilkins, Audio Research Corporation, Dayton

---

[10] In the 1970s, the audio classified ads in the *Sunday LA Times* was the
can't-miss place for audiophiles in Southern California for new dealers,
equipment coming to stores, events, sales and also used equipment.

Michael Kuller

Wright, Gale speakers (sideways on stands with the chrome ends) and a few others. I bought their first Dahlquist electronic crossover as soon as they had one. Talking with owner Dick Hardesty one day, I asked what he thought were the best speakers available at the time.[11] He said, "I don't really know, but this guy says he does," handing me a copy of an "underground" audio magazine (not available on newsstands), *The Absolute Sound* (*TAS*). It was issue #6. He flipped to the Editor's Choice, where the editor, Harry Pearson (HP), had listed the KLH 9 electrostatic speakers and stacked Advents as the best speakers. How cool. I immediately subscribed with issue #7 and ordered the back issues as well. After reading *TAS,* and HP's Recommended Components, I sent my Dahlquist electronic crossover to be modified by Frank Van Alstine.

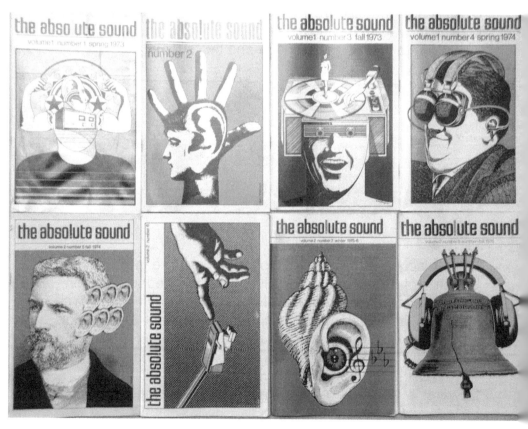

---

[11] Hardesty went on to found the *Audio Perfectionist Journal* and even write an article or two for *TAS* in the 1990s.

The Lucky Audiophile: Anecdotes from High-End Audio

Hardesty told me that he liked the new B & W DM-6 speakers (nicknamed "pregnant penguins") which they had just received. He had bought a pair for himself.

B&W DM-6 Speakers

I recall going into the store one day and hearing Hardesty auditioning a new ARC amp (D-350?) with Boz Scaggs' "Harbor Lights" and pronouncing the amp as the best he'd heard. Another time, I came in and the big Dayton Wright electrostats (filled with an inert gas and hermetically sealed) were in the lobby of the store playing CS&N's "Shadow Captain."

Richard Hardesty from his *TAS* tribute after his passing at 70 in 2014

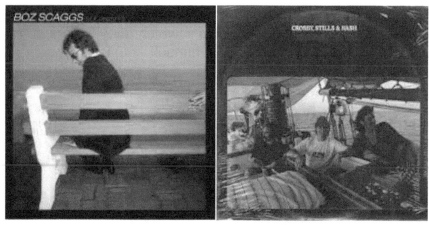

Dayton Wright XG-8 Electrostatic Speakers

Now I needed a preamplifier to complete my system. I was in Jonas Miller's high-end audio salon in LA and was talking to the salesperson about preamps. I asked him if he knew anything about the Rappaport PRE-1 (which had won *The Audio Critic*'s shootout of about 20 current preamps in issue #1). The salesperson said he had heard it but preferred the John Curl-designed Levinson JC-2 preamp, which came in at #2 in that shootout. Then he said he had purchased a Rappaport preamp and it was in his car out back. He wanted to sell it, so we could go take a look at it if I wanted. We went out to the parking lot, and I bought it from him. Talk about good fortune.

Rappaport PRE-1 Preamplifier

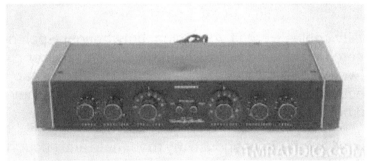

Dahlquist DQ-LP1 Electronic Variable Low Pass Filter

Based on the reviews I read, I bought a Kenwood KD500 turn-table and a Black Widow arm for my ADC-XLM II cartridge. I had read HP really liked the original XLM.

Kenwood KD-500 Turntable with Infinity Black Widow Tonearm

Polk Cobra Speaker Cables

Specialty cables weren't yet a thing, but I bought a pair of Fulton interconnects and two pair of Polk Cobra speaker cables. They were more expensive and fancier than the cheap interconnects and lamp-cord speaker cable, so I figured they must sound better.

The small two-bedroom house my roommate and I bought that year had a detached double garage with a concrete-slab floor and cinderblock walls that had been converted into a family room. It had an open beam ceiling, carpet, a fireplace and French doors that opened to a patio by the dining room. This became my music room. I furnished it with my system and a single couch. We sat on the couch to listen and there was actually a stereo image. Music was no longer just for the background, but for really listening. I was listening to music like most people watch TV. So here I was in early 1978 with a near-state-of-the-art audio system, at least according to *The Audio Critic*'s first issue, in a dedicated music room. It was musical bliss. Jackson Browne had come out with his *Pretender* album, Steely Dan with their masterpiece, *Aja,* Fleetwood Mac with *Rumours,* and Linda Ronstadt with *Simple Dreams.*

In *The Audio Critic*'s second issue, editor Peter Aczel dumped the Dahlquist system for his reference and said he preferred the new Rogers' LS3/5a, a small English bookshelf speaker, still popular today. I went and auditioned them at a new store in an LA business park (*LA Times* classifieds again) and thought they were cute, musical and imaged very well, but weren't nearly as good as my system.

Rogers LS3/5a Speaker

At one point, changing cartridges on my Black Widow tonearm, I broke the connector off of the tiny tonearm wire. I called Infinity and they said to bring it in and they would repair it for me. They weren't far away, in the San Fernando Valley, so I dropped it by late one afternoon. When I entered the lobby, I saw a protype speaker. The guy there told me it was their new Infinity QRS speaker, a bass box with a ribbon midrange and tweeters on movable panels to aim them.

Infinity QRS Speakers

Later, HP at *TAS* would combine these ribbon panels with the Magneplanar Tympani 1-D bass panels for his ideal speaker of the day he called the QRS-1D in *TAS*.

QRS-1D Hybrid Speakers

Reading the *Sunday LA Times* stereo ads, I found another audio store in Santa Ana I hadn't noticed before. I drove down to check it out. Led Zeppelin's *Physical Graffiti* album was their latest; a guy in the store, a regular who hung out there, was listening to it on one of their systems, saying how great he thought the album was. I listened to a pair of Acoustat X electrostatic speakers that had been reviewed in *TAS* and

found out what they meant by the "venetian blind ef
speakers sounded good but if you moved your r
sound changed.

Acoustat X Speakers

Harry Pearson of *TAS* and J. Gordon Holt of *Stereophile*
Photo by Bill Reckert

A few words about the audio press: Of the numerous main-
stream audio publications in these days, *Audio, Stereo Review* and *High Fidelity* were probably the most popular. J. Gordon Holt had been a writer and technical editor for *High Fidelity* and got frustrated that the magazine seemed only interested in technical measurements of the components they reviewed and paid no attention to the way they sounded. So in
about 1962, he left and started *Stereophile,* envisioned as a

quarterly journal focused on describing how the components actually sounded playing music. He and his wife did all of the work so the magazine's publishing schedule was very erratic and unpredictable. In 1972, Harry Pearson, a writer for *Newsday,* got frustrated with *Stereophile*'s publishing schedule and decided to start his own publication, *The Absolute Sound.* Then in 1977, Peter Aczel, who had been an audio ad copywriter, started *The Audio Critic.*

The 1970s were the birth of *high-end* audio, a term Harry Pearson copyrighted and popularized (but didn't invent). High-end audio was equipment designed to reproduce music as faithfully as possible, usually from specialized small US manufacturers in contrast to the popular mass-produced Japanese solid-state rack systems that didn't really reproduce recorded music very well. It wasn't just about price, because some fairly inexpensive equipment qualified for high end as well as the higher priced gear. Harry wrote about the top equipment of the day and the people behind the products, like Arnie Nudell of Infinity, Jim Winey of Magneplanar and William Johnson of Audio Research. He really brought it to life.

Ironically, none of these publications were able to make it out quarterly, so sometimes 6 months passed between issues. Audiophiles were craving more to read and were frustrated because the issues came out so late with so long in between. *TAS* was the most well written, controversial and exciting of the underground audio publications. I remember when a new issue of *TAS* would arrive, I would be so thrilled I would have trouble sleeping that night.

Chapter Three
The Later Years

I moved to Oakland, CA, in the summer of 1978 to take a job in hospital pharmacy management. This was a very fortunate move because the audio and music scenes were hopping in San Francisco at the time. At a San Francisco audio store, I met a couple of audiophiles, and I would get together with them to listen to some of the latest equipment. The one whose small house in SF we hung out at had a pair of Sound Labs Renaissance Electrostatic speakers sitting on a pair of RH Labs subwoofers. He had his equipment and turntable in the next room to prevent vibrations and the loud sound from affecting them. He knew tubed-audio designer Bruce Moore (Paragon preamplifier) who lived close by and he was always trying out his latest preamp designs. One of the demo cuts we used over and over in that era was "Keep Your Eye on the Sparrow," from the Dave Grusin Sheffield direct-to-disc recording, *Discovered Again*. It is an excellent recording of a small jazz combo (excellent musicians, too) with very lifelike drum and instrument sounds; it sounded terrific on his system.

RH Labs Subwoofer

In 1978 I was fortunate to see Little Feat play in Berkeley while Lowell George was still with the band (he died the next summer of a heart attack). Great band and terrific performance. *Waiting for Columbus* was recorded in 1977 and released in 1978.

That same year, I happened to see an article in *New West* magazine, a California lifestyle publication of all places, written by James Boyk called "The Perfectly Complete, Completely Perfect Thinking Person's Guide to Stereos." Still available on the Internet, it described in detail how to buy a stereo system and what to listen for and went on to suggest some used equipment to consider, like the original Quad speakers. It was one of the best articles I had seen on the topic. Boyk was an accomplished pianist who was a lecturer in music and electrical engineering at Cal Tech, teaching Projects in Music and Science. He was a very interesting guy and founded Performance Recordings.

The Club

In 1979, one of the SF audiophiles, Gary, and I decided we should start an audio hobbyist group and we founded the Northern California Audio Society (NCAS). The only other audio club we knew about was the Boston Audio Society. We put ads in the San Francisco Chronicle audio classified section and also advertised in the back of *Audio maga*zine. Our promotional stuff said, "Learn About Audio in the '80s!" I wrote the monthly newsletter on my typewriter, starting out with two pages, about our last event (we called them "events" instead of meetings) and what the next event would be. As I added more information from some of our listening, new equipment I heard would be coming into the retail stores and what the underground audio publications were saying, it expanded to as much as seven pages. The other founder, who was more artistic, was in charge of our quarterly journal, which was well done but usually late. At our height we had 300 members. I did a lot of copying, stamping and mailing.

Since I was writing a column in the newsletter discussing the latest reviews from *TAS, Stereophile, International Audio Review,* I put their editors on our mailing list. Peter Moncrieff of *IAR* was living in Berkeley at the time and came to some of our NCAS meetings. I would get pithy postcards from HP in red ink if he disagreed with something I wrote about *TAS.*

I remember visiting Peter Moncrieff's apartment one day with Gary. It was upstairs, just off of Telegraph Ave., in a big apartment building near UC Berkeley. In the entry was a pile of electronic parts and scraps, including a TV picture tube. (I had heard that Moncrieff had kept some speakers he had been sent for review and had taken them apart to build his own speakers.) In his dark narrow apartment was a single old beat-up red stuffed chair against the back wall and a couple of black Acoustat 2s on either side of a window about 8 to 10 feet way. On either side of the speakers and lining the walls of the entire room were racks of LPs, three levels high made out 2 X 4s. *IAR* was an interesting publication because the first few issues were thick, large-format magazines and read almost like textbooks about audio. In one of them, he recommended capacitive loading for moving magnet phono cartridges, with a list and recommendations. After those big issues, *IAR* became a monthly newsletter. Later, Moncrieff began publishing his newsletter on red paper so it couldn't be photocopied and shared, but it was pretty hard to read. After a few red issues, he went back to regular paper. Moncrieff was an interesting guy. He was pretty softspoken, but obviously very knowledgeable. If you asked him what he thought about a particular component, he would always respond by asking you what you thought about it, not wanting to sound too opinionated. But in *IAR* he had very strong opinions. He did come up with a couple of good hyperbolic descriptions for comparing audio components that got my attention. There was "All other CD players are boat anchors compared to this one" and my favorite, "This Oracle Delphi turntable is 634 times better than the Linn [Sondek turntable] and that's a scientific fact."

I was working in Berkeley when, on a hot summer day, I saw Moncrieff, a big guy, riding a ten-speed bike wearing shorts, a t-shirt and fur earmuffs. I guess they were to protect his hearing so he could focus on the "trebles," as he called them, in his listening.

Over the next few years, I upgraded my system. First I sold the Rappaport preamp and bought a new Threshold NS-10.

Threshold NS-10 Preamplifier

Then I traded out the Quatre amplifiers and bought a used Threshold 400a for the Dahlquists and a used Bryston 4B for the Dahlquist subwoofers, which I then traded out for a pair of new RH Labs subs. Things were sounding better.

Threshold 400a Amplifier

Bryston 4B Amplifier

I bought my first moving-coil cartridge, a Denon 103D. Later on I bought a Koetsu cartridge, which I thought sounded in-credible—warm, rich and lifelike.

Original Koetsu MC Cartridge

Then I began modifying the DQ-10s[12] The biggest weakness of the speakers was the cheap piezoelectric tweeter that crossed over above the regular tweeter to extend the high fre-quencies. I bought a kit from an ad in the back of *Audio* mag-azine with KEF T-27 tweeters and resistors to replace the two stock tweeters and the tweeter-level pot. This is the same tweeter used in the Rogers LS3/5a speaker.

KEF T-27 Tweeter

---

[12] The Dahlquist DQ-10s, it turns out were designed by Jon Dahlquist with his business partner Saul Marantz (after selling Marantz to Superscope) and then finally voiced in Harry Pearson's listening room (of *The Absolute Sound*) with his help.

Rear of DQ-10

Fortunately, the DQ-10s had an open architecture, with the crossover exposed on the back that made modifications easy. I continued the mods with a new set of polypropylene capacitors to replace most of the mylar caps in the crossover and then crossed them over with smaller ones. I swapped out all the internal wiring in the speaker to Monster Cable and put felt on the front baffles around the speakers. I wrote a letter to *TAS* detailing all my modifications and, to my surprise, they printed it as a one-page article. I was published!

Eventually, I swapped the NS-10 preamp for a used Audio Research SP-6B with a wooden enclosure, my first tubed component. It sounded like real music to me, and I loved it.

Audio Research SP-6B Preamplifier

Michael Kuller

I also picked up a pair of thick Fulton Gold speaker cables that looked like they came from supporting the Bay Bridge.

Fulton Gold 4AWG Speaker Cable

Next I picked up a used Threshold Stasis 2 and sold the 400a. I was in hi-fi heaven.

Threshold Stasis 2 Amplifier

One of our friends in NCAS was going to San Francisco State University, so we were able to get large rooms for our meetings. At one meeting I recall, we did a blind comparison of three loudspeakers of different sizes (small medium and large) behind an acoustically transparent sheet. Attendees guessed which was which and voted on the one they liked best. We unveiled them and most of the people were surprised. Another event was an afternoon open house for us at Leo De Gar Kulka's Golden State recording studio in SF.

We were invited to Garland Audio in San Jose one evening to hear the debut of David Wilson's large new WAMM speakers.

Wilson Audio Modular Monitor Speaker (WAMM)

Eventually, we moved our meetings to UC Berkeley since the Berkeley Fire Marshal was one of our members and could get us rooms and lecture halls there. Here are some highlights:

- William Johnson of ARC came and talked to us about his mostly tubed electronics that were considered state of the art.

- Leonard Norwitz, a school teacher that someone knew, came and did a great presentation on "How to Listen to Music." Norwitz later became the Audio Note US sales rep and brought an Ongaku Amplifier ($60,000) to my house in the 1990s for me to write about. He also wrote a couple of articles for Enjoy The Music.Com.

- Bill Ruck was the chief engineer for radio station KFOG in SF and came to talk to us. The station had just switched formats from easy listening (with the foghorn) to classic rock. Ruck was inducted into the Bay Area Radio Hall of Fame in 2014.

- We invited Threshold designer Nelson Pass to come speak at a meeting at my house where we also did a wine tasting. He's a very interesting character and we all had a great time.

Nelson Pass

One of our active members was Art Ferris and, from time to time, we hung out at his house and did listening sessions with his Dahlquist DQ-10s and two larger, coffin-sized RH Labs subwoofers. He eventually founded The Audible Illusions Corporation and took a Bruce Moore design for a small tubed pre-amplifier and turned it in to the Modulus Preamp. By now, he has sold nearly 20,000 of them.

I recall meeting Enid Lumley at a get-together at his house. About 6ft tall and very imposing, she was a sweet, soft-spoken woman. She wrote a controversial column for *TAS* describing things that affected the sound that verged on the supernatural. Later, she wrote a couple of columns for Peter Moncrieff in his *IAR* Newsletter.

Enid Lumley

I also met Dr. Larry Greenhill there. He was a member of the Westchester Audiophile Society in New York and went on to write a controversial double-blind cable comparison article for *Stereo Review* in 1983. He then wrote for a publication called *High Performance Review,* which took a little more scientific approach to evaluating audio equipment. He finally went to *Stereophile* where he still writes reviews today.

Bruce Brisson was a local audiophile who had helped us with a project to try to understand cable sound. His handmade interconnects were terrific, and I bought a pair from him. Then he started a new company, Music Interface Technologies or MIT, to produce cables. We got a pair of his Music Hose (MH)-750 speaker cables to audition and were very impressed. He later went to work for Monster Cable in SF for a short time, as it seemed many of the local audiophiles did. His Shotgun MIT interconnect cables came into demand after HP started using them in his system.

Michael Kuller

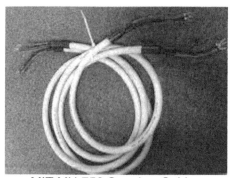

MIT MH-750 Speaker Cables

Another active member was Allen Hardy, a BMW importer and repair-shop owner who became the US importer for van den Hul products. He was living high up in the Berkeley Hills in Country Joe McDonald's old brick house, and we used to visit him and listen to his dual pair of KLH 9 Electrostats. Allen brought a pair of van den Hul Monitor speakers to an NCAS meeting to demo for us. I thought they sounded great, so I later bought a pair of them. Eventually I sold the speakers to my next door neighbor. When his wife saw them, she said, "Get those butt-ugly speakers out of my living room." Now we talk about WAF, wife acceptance factor. They divorced a few years later.

van den Hul Monitor Speakers (there's a rear-firing tweeter on the angled back panel). They did have covers that went over the top so you didn't see the drivers.

Then I picked up an EMT cartridge and had him send it to van den Hul to retip with his micro-ridge stylus and remove the body. It sounded really good.

Nude van den Hul EMT Cartridge

I was using a Conrad-Johnson Premier Two preamp at this time, but a short occurred and it blew out one of the van den Hul's woofers. I took the preamp to DB Audio for repair and they were unable to find anything wrong. So I hooked it back up and blew out another of the speaker's woofers. Since the replacement woofers weren't easy to get and took a while, I told the guys at DB this wasn't going to work. So they swapped out my Premier Two for a new PV-5 preamp, and I used it for a couple of years.

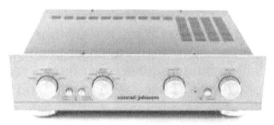

Conrad-Johnson PV-5 Preamplifier

Back in college, in 1967, when the new James Bond spoof film, *Casino Royale*, came out, I went to see it and liked the Tijuana Brass soundtrack with Dusty Springfield, so I picked up the LP, probably for $3.98. I lost track of the album and then, in the 1980s after reading HP's praise for Dusty singing "The Look of Love," I went to a used record store and bought a copy for $50. I'm sure it's worth much more now. It's a great recording, a terrific song and full of fun music.

Michael Kuller

In the early 1980s, some interesting things were happening at some of the underground audio publications. *The Audio Critic* stopped publishing after nine or ten issues. In their last issue, Peter Aczel gave a rave review to a new loudspeaker called the Fourier 1. He failed to mention that it was made by a company he owned. When the speaker came out, I went down and listened to it. It was a three-way speaker in a box and didn't seem to do anything special. It upset me that he wasn't refunding any of the subscription money we had all sent him. So one Saturday afternoon, when I was working on the NCAS newsletter, I got his telephone number from directory assistance in Bronxville, NY, and called him. He answered the phone, and I told him I was a charter subscriber from NCAS and was writing an article about him and the speakers. I asked him why he didn't mention in his review that it was his loudspeaker. He said he didn't own the entire company (I think his wife owned half) and he began to get angry. I asked him why he hadn't refunded the subscribers' money and asked if that was what he used to fund his new loudspeaker company. He cursed at me and hung up.

Fourier 1 speakers

After a few years, Aczel's Fourier Company went out of business. A few years after that, he got some funding and resumed publishing *The Audio Critic.* He offered to continue anyone's subscription he owed issues to, but only if you found out, wrote and asked him. But this time his attitude was very different. Since he had lost his credibility, he started bashing the other audio publications and focusing on measurements and double-blind tests for proof of audible differences. From a guy who did a very "subjective" comparison and ranking of 20 preamplifiers in his first issue, he became a hardened objectivist and the reviewer everyone loved to hate.

In 1980, Walt Jung and Richard Marsh wrote a two-part article in *Audio* magazine about the different capacitors used in audio equipment and how they affect the sound. Peter Moncrieff of *IAR* was all over this. He later came out with his own brand of audio capacitors, IAR Wonder Caps, and called them "the world's best sounding capacitors." He continued to publish *IAR,* consult with manufacturers and give great reviews to equipment, which he mentioned used his Wonder Caps (like ARC at the time). He eventually stopped publishing *IAR* and put it online (IAR-80). The last I heard, Moncrieff was living in a castle outside of San Diego and driving a Porsche.

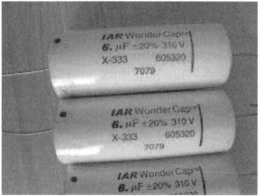

IAR Wonder Caps

Stereophile continued to struggle with its publishing schedule and Larry Archibald, a businessman, purchased it in 1982. He expanded the staff and brought John Atkinson over from England's *Hi-Fi News* to be the editor, although J. Gordon Holt stayed on and continued to write reviews.

Peter Moncrieff, John Atkinson, Larry Archibald and Harry Pearson

Michael Kuller

I continued my audio odyssey of listening to the latest and greatest equipment. Audio Excellence in San Francisco got in Hill Plasmatronics floor-standing speakers with plasma tweeters, powered by a refillable tank of helium inside the speaker box. When they played, you could see a very bright little light inside the rectangle above the speaker grille, which was the corona arc of the plasma tweeter. The high frequencies sounded great, but it seemed impractical for home use.

Hill Plasmatronics Speaker

Audio Excellence was also the first place I listened to the MartinLogan CLS Electrostats. They were very transparent in more ways than one.

MartinLogan CLS Electrostats

I was in San Diego and stopped by Audio Dimensions, a store owned by Ike Eisenstadt who wrote a monthly newsletter called *Audio Update.* I didn't get to meet him, but I did get to hear a pair of big Beveridge Electrostats, which were positioned facing each other with about six feet between them. In that space they created a big, very specific image. The salesman played Willie Nelson's *Stardust* album for me, and I swear I could see Willie right there in the middle singing.

Beveridge Electrostatic Speakers

A new high-end audio equipment store called Fidelis opened in a Victorian House in San Francisco. A friend took me there, and I met the owner, Tim Marutani, who still consults today. In a large room he had the Levinson HQD system. It consisted of stacked original Quad speakers, two 24-inch Hartley subwoofers and a pair of Decca Tweeters. The speakers were driven by six Levinson ML-2 amplifiers, three per side. They sounded pretty amazing. Marutani eventually moved Fidelis into a retail space near Fisherman's Wharf. There, I saw one of the first Krell amplifiers (a new Mark Levinson challenger), the Fourier 1 speaker and Goldmund's latest equipment.

Levinson HQD System

I heard that Jon Dahlquist was going to be introducing his new speakers at The Audible Difference, a high-end audio store in Palo Alto. They were his DQM series of box speakers, with the drivers made by Magnat in Germany with the box enclosures made there in Germany, too. They sounded ok, but I sure expected more. We were having an Audio Society meeting that night so I thought I'd ask Jon if he could come talk to us. David Wilson was also there. David had been an engineer at Cutter Labs in Berkeley. The company made sterile IV solutions for hospitals and equipment to administer them. Wilson had begun making speakers to monitor the recordings he was making. Unfortunately, I found that Wilson had already invited Dahlquist to dinner so they could discuss speaker design. Later that afternoon, I overheard Dahlquist tell him, "The most important thing is to get the lower midrange right, because if you do, everything else will fall into place."

Dahlquist DQM-9 Speakers

I called James Boyk, of Performance Recordings, at Cal Tech and interviewed him for a two-part article in the NCAS newsletter. His 1978 article on how to buy stereo equipment had been a finalist for the National Magazine Awards and he had some very interesting opinions on music and technology.

John Curl and his buddy, Brian Cheney, of VMPS speakers, shared a small office in Berkeley on College Ave. across from the Elmwood Theater. We stopped in to chat with them a couple of times. I went to Brian's VMPS showroom in El Cerrito to get something from him, probably a pair of cables. The large space was very impressive with his big speakers and a lot of sound deadening in the front part of the big room around them. He told me he liked the live-end–dead-end concept for room acoustics.

John Curl

Brian Cheney and Jim Bongiorno of Ampzilla (and Sumo) holding a
Manley Amplifier

I had really enjoyed helping run the audio society and writing about audio, but I had to leave NCAS in 1982 after getting married (very lucky), building a house and starting a business.[13] There just weren't enough hours in the day.

I used to buy equipment from DB Audio in Berkeley and hang out there from time to time. A lot of their salesmen went on from there to work for high-end audio manufacturers. Doug Blackwell, the owner, sold the store and went to work for Transparent Audio Marketing, John Hunter and Stirling Trayle took over Sumiko (distributing REL and Sonus Faber), Garth Leerer founded Musical Surroundings, and the younger new guy, Peter Bohacek, went to work for Avalon speakers, with Charles Hansen in Boulder.

John Hunter   Stirling Trayle

In 1982, we saw Paul Simon with Ladysmith Black Mambazo on their *Graceland* tour. It was a great show and one of my favorite albums of the 1980s. I highly recommend the documentary of its making, "Under African Skies."

We also saw a lot of terrific music at the Greek Theater in Berkeley that summer, which is still one of my favorite music venues. We saw Yes, The Police, Brian Ferry and the Eurythmics. The concert I think we enjoyed the most was Pat

---

[13] It was one of the first home-infusion pharmacies in the Bay Area. Timing and luck is everything: In 1983, Medicare changed their cost-plus hospital reimbursement to diagnostic related groups, flat payments encouraging patient discharge and home care. In the mid-1980s, AIDs hit the Bay Area. In 1989, five national companies were interested in buying us.

Michael Kuller

Metheny , Lyle Mays and Nana Vasconcelos, the Brazilian percussionist. Their music just seemed to float in the air over us on a warm night there. It was magical.

In 1982, I had heard Stevie Ray Vaughan on the radio when his first album came out and was fortunate to see him in the small Keystone Berkeley Club. Vaughan, who left us way too soon, had played guitar on David Bowie's *Let's Dance* album and was supposed to tour with him on his "Serious Moonlight Tour" promoting that album. Instead, he left to tour and promote his own album, *Texas Flood.* Mitch Woods and his Rocket 88s opened the show and then Vaughan blew everyone away with his guitar playing. I recall saying during his encore cover of "Voodoo Child, Revisited," "Wow, he's channeling Jimi Hendrix!"

In the early 1980s, a close friend decided to get married to his girlfriend in Reno during a ski trip with six of us at South Lake Tahoe. The Diamonds ("Little Darlin'" and "The Stroll") were playing in one of the small showrooms at a casino there, so we went to see them on two successive nights. A few months later, their bass singer passed away. On a Caribbean cruise ship in about 2003, I saw Diamond Dave Sommerville, their lead singer, perform with Gary Duncan of Quicksilver Messenger Service on back-up vocals and piano in a theater on the ship. Dave sang all their songs and told a lot of great stories about the tour buses they were on in the 1950s and 1960s with Buddy Holly & The Crickets, Fats Domino, The Everly Brothers, and Chuck Berry.

Chapter Four

Where in the World is John

In 1982, John Iverson came out with his Electron Kinetics Eagle 7a power amplifier. It was supposed to have the best bass reproduction around, so I bought one in 1983. It weighed 110lb and had 350w/ch @ 8 ohms. A real monster. The next year, Iverson came out with the Eagle 2a, only 120w/ch @ 8 ohms, which was said to be a better sounding amplifier in just about every way and was less expensive.

Eagle 7a

Eagle 2a

John Iverson

John Iverson was a very eccentric electronics genius, a controversial character and the stuff of legends.

At the age 18, Iverson was alleged to have designed the guidance system for the NASA Lunar Module.

He had worked for Marantz, then founded Electro Research, where he developed the A75 amplifier, an incredible solid-state unit made for military radar installations, with a few left over for consumers. Harry Pearson called it one of the ten most significant amplifiers of all time. Iverson was working on a strain gauge cartridge/preamplifier and some other pretty esoteric stuff. Then he founded Electron Kinetics to make more cost-effective products for consumers. I'm told he used to personally deliver the Electron Kinetics amplifiers in the trunk of his Cadillac.

Iverson said he had invented a "force field" loudspeaker at Electro Research but had to dismantle it because it was too dangerous. This is an account in Copper Magazine (issue 119) from Frank Doris, when he was the set-up man for HP at TAS and was introduced to Iverson at a Consumer Electronics Show.

Someone introduced me to him. He did not need much prompting to begin talking and quickly started delving into some pretty esoteric stuff, to the point where those around us politely drifted away. Not me.

At one point I asked him what the best speaker he ever heard was. He brightened up and said, "No question about it—the plasma speaker." I replied, "You mean the Hill Plasmatronics?" He scoffed and said something along the lines of, "No, not that thing! I'm talking about an experimental full-range speaker that I worked on. It makes every other speaker sound like a joke. However, it can't be put into production."

I asked, "Why not," thinking it would involve large tanks of helium gas, high voltages, oxygen depletion or outrageous expense. Iverson replied, "It's too dangerous."

"What could be so dangerous?" Iverson looked me straight in the eye. "One time we were listening to the speakers and a fly flew into the room. Then the fly flew between the speakers … and disappeared."

Had I heard that right? "The fly disappeared?"

"Yes. I think the fly flew into another dimension. Somehow the loudspeakers created a gateway into another dimension."

Wow! That sounds like a Vincent Price movie to me.

Here is a first-person account of listening to Iverson's speaker (from The What's Best Forum posted by Mobiusman in February 2017).

First, let me set the scene. We all arrived at the same time to the non-descript business park in northern Orange County, CA. When we entered, it was even more ramshackle than any of us expected for such a fabled product, although in retrospect considering other previous meetings with Iverson, this is exactly what we should have expected, since he did not care about what others thought of him.

The speakers were approximately the size of Dayton Wrights seemingly somewhat randomly set up, although they had to be, from a phase perspective, very carefully set up. There was a crappy chair in the listening position (about 15–20 feet from the speakers/transducers) with a patched large hole in the wall behind the listening position where allegedly the speakers blew a hole in the wall. There was a power supply about 30" cubed connected to the speakers with a huge (1–2" diam) power cable that was allegedly directly tapped into the facility's custom large electrical transformers.

I was the first to listen to some of Iverson's records played through a custom Iverson preamp/phono stage driven by his Electro Research power supply and another similar power supply driving a Panasonic Strain Gauge cartridge. I do not remember the turntable other than it was incredible.

The beam of sound was just that, a beam with incredible reduction of power even an inch off axis. In the beam was something I would expect had I been abducted by aliens, meaning it was unworldly. It reminded me of my memories of being under the influence of ether when 5 years old for a tonsillectomy, an experience I also remember as if it was yesterday because of the weirdness of the feeling. John claimed that even the deaf could hear the sound when sitting where I was, which led me to believe that I was sitting in a high RF field, also supported by the size of the power supply and its power cable. This also helps explain why I was neurologically very wrong the next day, suffering from a 2 day receptive aphasia where although I could understand words spoken to me, I was unable to put them together in a reasonable manner to make sense of their combination. I was a second year psychiatry resident at the time and made the mistake of going to work the next day, where my co residents thought I was psychotic when I relayed this story to the point that I had to run out or have possibly been committed. On my way home I almost caused an accident when I turned in front of an oncoming policeman that I did not see. Fortunately, I was able to get off because I was an "overworked resident at USC"!

I will use a term that is way overused on this forum and throughout audio, but I have no alternative—it was like "being there" with an extra sense that the entire experience was somewhat "velvety," while "melting" around the edges. I know this sounds strange, but I am just reporting what I remember. We listened to many cuts, with me listening way more than Marty and Steve who spent more time talking to John. Of the cuts I listened to was one that only a few have ever heard because it was a Ken Kreisel test pressing of his grandfather singing in an ice rink with the rink organ playing in the background, called Grandpa Sings. It was like doing drugs and listening to music, only to hear it later and realize that the difference was me. I still have that pressing and periodically listen to it to realize how different (plain) it sounds on my fairly substantial system.

I truly believed I was there, until I moved out of the beam and realized where I was. I conducted this experiment several times with the same results. John realized that something weird was going on with me and started questioning me with great enthusiasm, I suspect because he realized that I was truly letting myself go and thus less skeptical about his achievement.

I tried to shift the conversation to the military aspects of his amp and the force fields, but he became visibly very scared and then angry and told me that as much as he would like to talk about these subjects, he could not and was also fearful about doing so. (I swear he said this and no, I am not psychotic).

I do not remember much more probably for the following reasons—I believe that the system was emitting high levels of RF which is known to cause temporary neurologic problems like what I experienced.

Amazing! What a hobby, this audio and music reproduction! They say music is a time machine.

Here's another first-person account from the What's Best Forum written by Duke LeJeune in February 2020.

My Electron Kinetics Eagle 2 had a wonky on/off switch, so I called John. Apparently the FBI had recently confiscated his loudspeaker and all of his design notes. He was quite upset. My recollection is that he had filed a patent application and, in response, the FBI showed up. He told me they had accused him of stealing secrets from the Strategic Defense Initiative ("Star Wars") missile defense program. This was my first and only conversation with John and to say that he was colorful and animated and enthusiastic would be a huge understatement.

Iverson also claimed that an electronic tracking system he developed was stolen by the FBI. He ranted and raved about the FBI and the government, who he thought was monitoring him after that.

Iverson mysteriously disappeared in 1992 and is still listed as a missing person in Lake Havasu, NV. No one has heard from him since then.

Was he abducted by aliens? Sucked into a forcefield with that fly? Kidnapped by the government? Murdered by the FBI? There are guesses and theories all over the Internet, but no one knows for sure.

We now return control of your television set back to you for our regularly scheduled programming.

Back to Reality

We went to the Napa County Fair during the summer of 1983 and the Beach Boys happened to be playing there. We watched the small outdoor concert on bleachers with the whole band including Carl and Dennis (who drowned a few months later after a diving accident), and of course with Bruce Johnston instead of Brian.

Beach Boys

I decided I needed a new turntable so I bought a highly rated Linn Sondek, a belt-driven unit with a suspended subchassis, along with an Ittok arm. There was a lot of mystery surrounding its proper setup in those days, but a knowledgeable friend helped me do it. After realizing the Linn was very sensitive to foot falls in my second-story listening room, I tried to figure out a better way to stabilize it. Linn recommended a lower-mass table under it but that didn't work very well. So I ended up suspending it from my ceiling on a plywood platform, held by heavy gauge fishing line. That worked.

Linn Sondek Turntable with Ittok Arm

A friend told me Mark Levinson was going to record a Stan Getz concert at the Keystone Club in San Francisco. My wife and I went and had seats close to the front in the center of the small club. I was able to go downstairs to look at Levinson's recording equipment. Since the *Getz/Gilberto* album, Getz has always been one of my favorite jazz artists. He performed with Lou Levy on piano, Monty Budwig on bass and Victor Lewis on drums. It was terrific and became *The Dolphin*.

Ken Kessler, an entertaining American reviewer from the British *Hi-Fi News* magazine was travelling across America to check out the US audio scene which would be chronicled in an article for *Hi-Fi News*. John Hunter of DB Audio invited me over to his place—he was renting a room in a house in Berkeley. First we listened to his white Acoustat 1+1s on either side of his bed with "Hold Me Now" by the Thompson Twins. They sounded great. Then Kessler and another DB audio salesman came in. We chatted with them for a while, had a few laughs and they took off. I used to run into Kessler at the Consumer Electronic Shows in Las Vegas in the 1990s—once he opened his long coat, like a flasher, to reveal rows of classic watches he was selling lining the inside. He was always a colorful character.

Ken Kessler and Michael Fremer

Chapter Five
The Call

In 1985, out of the blue, I got a call from Harry Pearson. He asked me if I would like to write equipment reviews for *The Absolute Sound*. I couldn't believe it. My audio-writing dream had come true.

The premise of *The Absolute Sound* was to compare the sound of the audio equipment to live, unamplified music in a real space—the *absolute sound.* Over the years, this has become controversial since what you are really listening to for evaluating a product is a recording, not actual live music. Harry went on to create a list of "Super Discs," which he considered reference quality. Since critical listening is a learned skill, I had always thought that if you listened to enough live music, you would be able to recognize the additive and subtractive errors from the equipment.

TAS was based in Sea Cliff on Long Island in New York. Harry was a very insightful listener and writer. He is considered by many to be the most influential person in the history of audio journalism. Like Gordon Holt before him, he created many of the terms we use to describe what we're hearing with reproduced music. Some of the things he first described are *soundstaging, macro- and microdynamics, transparency, immediacy* and *image placement,* just to name a few.

My wife is from Philadelphia and has a big family (Her older brothers had been on *Bandstand* and one was at Woodstock.) so we go back there about once a year. I let Harry know we would be there so he invited us to Sea Cliff for dinner. We stopped at his house and he took us, along with another guy I don't recall, to the little French restaurant in Sea Cliff. He was well known there, so I assume that's where he takes everybody. After dinner, we went back to his house and listened to his huge IRS system in a 20' X 16' room. I remember he put on a Mercury orchestral recording first. The sound was overwhelming—incredibly big, powerful and realistic in that small room. It was as close to live music as I had heard. We listened with him for about an hour and the one song that I recall vividly was the British single from the Human League, "Don't You Want Me." He said, "There are seven layers to this song. If you listen, you can hear them come in one by one." And we listened and they did. It was an amazing experience and one of the highlights of my life, my wife and I listening with HP, as was seeing my first review in print.

Infinity IRS Speakers (not HP's room)

In about a year, I was back again at Sea Cliff for the weekend long *TAS* "staff meeting." I met most of the people in the photo, including John Nork, Steven Stone and Frank Doris.

Frank Doris
Photo by David Parvey

We had individual sessions about writing reviews with Harry in the third story turret of his house where he told me, "Remember to always illustrate your comment on the sound with a musical passage." We took turns, three at a time, listening to the latest iteration of his big IRS system. Afterward, Art Dudley, Frank Doris, and a few of us sat on his wraparound porch talking about it. Tom Miiller asked us, "What do you think is responsible for the big improvement in the sound I hear on Harry's system?" We all guessed. He said he thought it was the new Koetsu Signature phono cartridge.

HP's House at 176 Prospect Ave. in Sea Cliff, NY

TAS Staff Meeting. Back row—Jack Orbach, Art Dudley, Harry Pearson, Mike Kuller (me), Unknown, Tom Miiller, David Wilson, Dr. John Coolidge. Second row—Sallie Reynolds, Bob Reina, Andy Benjamin, Robert Greene, Kevin Conklin, Sheryl Lee Wilson, Unknown. Third row—Unknown, Brian Gallant, Fred Kaplan, Unknown, Tam Henderson. Fourth row—Unknown, Kevin Messmer, Roger Modjeski, Christina Yuin, Roger Kagan, Unknown, Unknown. Front—Jeff Goggin. Photo by Steven Stone.

I had never paid much attention to classical music before. A girlfriend took me to my first classical concert in Denver in 1972, our senior year in college. To write about the sound of audio equipment compared to "the absolute sound," I figured I needed to familiarize my ears with live, unamplified orchestral music, so we started going to symphonies at the Davies Symphony Hall in San Francisco in 1985. We sat behind the orchestra, on the side, in the Golden Circle (first balcony) and in the orchestra. Things sounded a little different from each area. In some we could hear the soloists or sections of the orchestra more clearly; in others the orchestra ensemble blended better. Up closer, the sound was bigger and more dynamic (HP had seats in the middle of the second row at Carnegie Hall). In 1986, I got season tickets—row P, center (not luck but a small donation to the symphony). These were terrific seats and we went to eight performances a year for the next two years. We saw some great performances from virtuosos like Itzhak Perlman, Isaac Stern and Andre Watts. But by then my wife and I had a daughter, had to get babysitters and were both still working full time, so it became too much and we gave the season tickets up.

Davies Symphony Hall from the Golden   Davies from the Stage

One day I got a call from, Jeff Goggin, who worked with HP setting up equipment and whom I had met at the staff meeting. He said he was going to be in the area and wanted to know if he could stay with me. We had an extra bedroom, so I invited him over. We listened to some music that night and, the next morning, he told me he was going to start a new high-end audio-review magazine called *Sounds Like ...* and wanted to know if I would be interested in joining him. Michael Gindi, Tom Miiller and Myles Astor (three *TAS* reviewers) were all in, he said. I told him I'd have to think about it. Here I was writing for the top audio publication in the US and was being mentored somewhat by guru Harry Pearson. Why would I want to jump to a new start-up magazine? I declined. The magazine folded after a couple of years.

I had been sent a pair of floor-standing speakers to review and wanted something to compare them to. I called Brian Cheney and asked him if I could borrow a not-too-big pair of his VMPS speakers. Brian was known for designing tall, coffin-like box speakers with great sound, excellent low bass and a really good value. He brought a pair of his smaller speakers over and set them up. Behind the speakers in the living room of our small 20' X 40' (two bedroom, 1600 sq ft) two-level house was a fireplace. He couldn't get the speakers to sound very good, but left them there anyway. I tried positioning them and the speakers never clicked with my room and system. A couple of days later Cheney called and asked if he could take them back so I figured that would be best. Maybe eight years later in the early 1990s, Cheney wrote an article for *Stereophile* magazine describing the advantages of live-end–dead-end room treatments. In it he said the worst room he had ever heard was one of a reviewer from another publication where the fireplace set rattled when the speakers played. Hey, I'm pretty sure he was talking about my room! Reading the article sitting in my newer, sound-treated, dedicated, purpose-built room, I was mortified that anyone might figure out it was my old room he was describing.

Early in my reviewing, *TAS* reviewer Robert Greene was in town and paid me a visit. He was a math professor at UCLA who played the violin. We did some listening and later I realized HP had probably sent him over to see if my system sounded any good and if I knew what I was doing. Later, when I was in southern California, I paid him a visit and listened to his system. We walked through his house and it seemed that just about every closet was filled with LPs. His listening room was his double garage and his system sounded very engaging. He played an older Doris Day record and her voice sounded terrific. I didn't know she had made records and looked for a copy locally, but I never found one.

In the later 1980s, I was sent a pair of floor-standing JSE Infinite Slope Model 2 speakers to review. They were designed by John Sollecito and used an Infinite Slope crossover designed by Richard Modafferi, an engineer with McIntosh. I really liked them, gave them a good review and bought the pair. The company went out of business some years later and in the 1990s, Jeff Joseph acquired the rights and designed his Joseph Audio speakers using the Infinite Slope crossovers. His speakers have become very successful and have always impressed me when I've heard them at shows.

JSE Model 2

Michael Kuller

Also in the later 1980s, Amanda McBroom put on a concert at Bimbo's Club in SF sponsored by Monster Cable, and I was invited. I had met Noel Lee around 1980 near DB Audio in his little Honda when he was starting Monster Cable. He seemed like a real wheeler-dealer. Now his company was much larger and he was very successful. Amanda's Sheffield Direct to Disk album, *Growing up in Hollywood Town,* was an audio demo chestnut, especially her cover of "The Rose." It was great to hear her sing live.

Over the years, the were a number of other audio review magazines have come and gone. These are the ones I recall. I'm sure there were many others.

Stereo Opus—edited by Tom Norton, who went on to write for *Stereophile* and is now with *Sound & Vision*

High Performance Review—edited by Larry Greenhill, now with *Stereophile*

Bound for Sound—written by Martin DeWulf

The Audio Perfectionist—Richard Hardesty

Audio Horizons—Len Hupp

The $ensible $ound—edited by John Horan

Listener—edited by Art Dudley, who later joined *Stereophile*

Audio Alternatives[14]—edited by Larry Greenhill, now with
  Stereophile

Ultimate Audio—edited by Myles Astor, now Senior Editor at
  Positive Feedback

Play (then *Press Play*)—Tom Miiller

Then there were some publications for the DIY audio hobby-
ists—*Speaker Builder, Audio Amateur* and *Audio X Press.*
And there were at least a half dozen British audio review publications, a few of which are still in business today.

Frank Doris, and then later Scot Markwell, performed very important functions for TAS. They were both great guys and very
easy to work with. Besides setting up Harry's equipment, pro-
curing equipment to review from the manufacturers and writing an occasional review themselves, they were the reviewers' interface with the magazine. That way, we didn't have to
bug Harry for every little thing. And for the most part, Harry
didn't have to deal directly with us. If we wanted to review
something we had heard or didn't want to review a component
we were sent or wanted to know where our latest check was,
or any other issues like this, we called them. They had to be
the two nicest and most patient guys in audio dealing with
Harry, all of these issues and some of the writers with big egos.

One of the best parts about living in Northern California and
writing for *TAS* was getting exposed to some of the great people in audio and music here.

- I was asked to go to a Berkeley loft to meet with Dr. Keith
  Johnson, computer whiz "Pflash" Pflaumer and Michael
  Ritter of Pacific Microsonics to write about a demo and

[14] This was an interesting publication. When it was first advertised, they
said they had taken out a $50,000 (or some big figure) bond to reimburse
subscribers if they ever stopped publishing, like so many other audio publications had. After a few years they stopped publishing. Some years later,
I noticed one of the principal reviewers on an internet newsgroup and
asked him about the bond. His response was, "I don't think anyone re-
membered about that but you."

the release of their new HDCD technology to make CDs sound better. While I was there I got to hear some of Dr. Johnson's amazing master tapes.

- Then I was asked to interview expert disc masterer Paul Stubblebine at the famous Hyde Street Studios in SF where many of the greatest classic rock albums were recorded and the album covers lined the walls. We talked about his work on the emerging CD surround sound, SACD and DVD-A technologies.

- I was also invited by Ed Wodenjak of Clarity Recordings to hear the recording of Schubert: Trio and Sonatina for Piano, Violin and Violincello played by Arturo Delmoni, Edward Auer and Nathaniel Rosen in the First United Church of Berkeley (it was actually in Kensington but the acronym wouldn't work). The album was to be a very simply miked recording with the mikes connected directly to a tape machine in the next room. I was able to listen through the headphones in that room as the mikes—one on each side of a thin wooden head cutout on a stand— were moved around to get the best sound. I could hear the placement and sound of each instrument as it changed.

Another advantage to living on the West Coast was being able to avoid all the politics and controversies. HP was a larger-than-life personality and the magazine was interesting because of all the controversies, characters and HP's strong opinions. Plus they covered all of the latest and greatest equipment. If a reader wrote a letter criticizing something in the magazine, HP would give a terse response that put him in his place. There was nothing like it in audio. He had his favorite writers, made some manufacturers mad and had a garage stacked full of audio equipment from manufacturers he hadn't gotten to, had forgotten about or had listened to but not returned. One of the best things about *TAS* was that most reviews had a second opinion or comment from another reviewer. This made some interesting interplay between the reviewers, particularly when they disagreed, like: "Cordesman, you ignorant slut!" Some of the reviewers claimed he pitted them against each other or played games with them, but I wasn't involved in any of that from my distance.

I had decided I wanted a new preamplifier, so I borrowed three different top solid-state units from DB Audio to audition—the Klyne (KL-7?), the Rowland Coherence One and possibly an Apt Holman, if I recall. After a few nights of comparative listening, I decided the Rowland sounded the best and bought one.

Not too long after that, HP called me and asked if I would do him a favor. David Wilson was writing a review of the Rowland Coherence One preamp and he asked if I would write a comment on it. Uh oh, this could be a setup. He also said if I wanted, he'd send me an Audio Research Corporation SP-10 tubed preamp (that he had rated the best) to compare. So I said, sure, I'd do it. Wilson wrote an extremely positive review of the Rowland. I wrote in my comment that, after comparing the two preamps, I found them both to be great. I used the Stan Getz Concert I attended and the Dolphin album as references. I said the Rowland took me back to my seats in the front with faster transients and a more forward, exciting sound. On the other hand, the SP-10 recreated all of the space of the club and put the combo a little further back. However, they both sounded very realistic to me. I could have happily lived with either one of them. I wrote exactly what I heard, and everyone was happy.

Rowland Coherence One Preamplifie

Audio Research SP-10 Preamplifier

Michael Kuller

DB Audio was great about loaning me equipment to use in comparisons. I always felt a review wasn't complete unless it was compared to something good in the same price range. I remember Stirling Trayle loaning me a pair of the new Apogee Caliper Ribbon Speakers to try out at home and never getting them to sound very good in my room with my system.

Apogee Caliper Ribbon Speakers

I had heard the earlier Thiel 03s and 04s at DB Audio and really liked them. Needing a new pair of speakers, I listened to the latest Thiel 3.5s with the bass equalizer. Designer Jim Thiel designed his speakers to have a flatter in-room high-frequency response, rather than rolled off high frequencies, so with the wrong equipment and placement, they could sound bright. I liked them, so I bought a pair.

In 1990, we built a new house, and, with a little help from a San Francisco acoustic engineer, we created a dedicated, nearly soundproof audio room. My wife was happy to finally get all the audio equipment out of the living room. Whenever we had people over for dinner, we always ended up in the music room. See Appendix II—MK's Listening Biases.

The pictures on the following pages were taken ten years later, around 2001 after I purchased my then-current "final system." Since the Thiel 7.2s could also sound a little bright, the Manley Neo Classic 250s and the impedance-matched MIT Oracle Cables seemed to balance everything well coming from the Wadia 850 CD player. The Wadia algorithm made the digital high frequencies sound better than most CD players and its digital volume control eliminated any need for a preamplifier. The system produced a big soundstage, focused imaging and a very musical sound. After Manley replaced their amplifier's transformers about the same time, a veil was lifted from the Neo Classic 250s sound and their bass sounded as good as any tubed amplifiers I had heard.

This is the view from my listening spot. The Thiel CS7.2s are nine feet from the front wall, 3.5' from the side walls, and ten feet from the listening spot which is eight feet from the back wall. The heavy lined drapes are mounted out six inches from the windows to provide a cushion of air. The ASC Tube Traps along the front bay windows are to reduce a 30Hz standing wave. The Argent Room Lenses help focus the image.

Michael Kuller

This is the right-rear view. The room is 27' X 17' X 10.5' high with a coffered ceiling. It is constructed with 2 layers of 5/8" sheetrock on offset studs. The floor is a concrete slab.

This is my built-in equipment closet. The Wadia 850 CD player is attached directly to the two Manley Neo-Classic 250 amps. The upper shelves were originally for my turntable and other digital equipment. There are five 20-amp dedicated circuits in the closet with hospital grade outlets.

Michael Kuller

This is the listening spot. Behind it are a couple of Room Tunes to absorb reflections from the French doors.

Besides this system, I also had a system in our family room for the TV sound: Vandersteen Model 2Ci speakers and lower-level Adcom electronics. The Vandersteens sounded pretty incredible for the money and became one of the top-selling speakers of all time. Later, I wrote a review of the Vandersteens for the magazine.

Vandersteen 2Ci Speakers

A new local company was making turntables that people were beginning to talk about, called SOTA (State of the Art). The company was started by Dave Fletcher (Sumiko) and Robert Becker. They hired Rodney Herman to work on the design and run the factory in Oakland. Their SOTA Sapphire was the first turntable to offer a vacuum record hold-down with an external pump to provide the suction. It was a belt-drive turntable with a sprung suspension and was supposed to improve upon the Linn Sondek's quirky design. I had decided I wanted one, so I went to the factory, back behind the Oakland Coliseum and met Rod Herman. He showed me around and introduced me to Allen Perkins,[15] who he had just hired from the East to help with the turntable's design. I talked with Allen briefly and watched him set up a smallish tubed amplifier in his office. He said it was an EAR, made by Tim de Paravicini, the renowned

---

[15] Allen later founded Immedia, which distributed Lyra cartridges and made RPM turntables.

Michael Kuller

British tube amplifier designer. In a couple of years, SOTA introduced a better model of their turntable, called the Cosmos. After talking with Rod, I decided not to switch to the new turntable but to just upgrade my platter to the Cosmos platter, which was much more well damped than the original. It was a noticeable improvement.

SOTA Star Sapphire Turntable

Compact Discs—Sony called them "Perfect Sound Forever"—came out in about 1985. CD players didn't make them sound very good at first, with their "brick wall filters" and "jitter," a digital distortion which wasn't identified until later. A few critics like HP continued to advocate for analog LPs and call CDs an abomination. He said, with LPs the distortion (pops, clicks, and hiss) are in the background, separate from the music. But with CDs, the distortion rides the music. By the mid-1990s, I had reviewed a couple of CD players, Teac's Esoteric, a Musical Concepts modified one that HP had liked and even a tubed D to A converter. They were making the CDs sound better and CDs were so much more convenient than records. With the remote control, you could play any song, skip ones you didn't like and play a whole album without having to get up at the half-way spot and turn it over. I realized I wasn't listening much to my LPs anymore. When I did listen to an LP, it did sound better but was much more of a pain. The record had to be cleaned before playing, the stylus needed cleaning and there was quite an involved setup for new cartridges. So I decided that If I really wanted to enjoy the sound of CDs, I shouldn't listen to records anymore. I put my turntable, record cleaning machine and all my records up for sale and sold them all over a weekend; I have never looked back. CD-player technology continued to improve and sound more and more musical.

The Audiophile Network (TAN) was the first audiophile internet newsgroup I recall. I first learned of it in the early 1990s. It was run by Guy Hickey, formerly of Quatre amplifiers. I can still hear the sounds my dial-up modem made to get on it. I wasn't very active but checked in from time to time to see what was going on.

I was once sent a pair of Dahlquist DQ-20s to review. They were reminiscent of the DQ-10s but were only a three-way system, with the drivers lined up on small baffles behind a cloth grille, designed by Carl Marchisotto.[16] The guy from Dahlquist came to set them up in my room and brought a frequency generator with a small printer to graph my room's sound. Surprisingly, there was a pretty big 30Hz standing wave along the front of the room and a smaller one at the rear but otherwise it was pretty good. Anyway, I had trouble getting the DQ-20s to sound very good. They sounded a little constipated and seemed to need more power to sound alive (like the DQ-10s had). I had just bought a pair of Brown Electronic Labs (BEL) 1001 amplifiers, which were 200w/ch @ 8 ohms used as mono amps. Tom Miiller had really liked these amps for all of their speed and the detail they revealed. HP had not been as impressed with them because their image was somewhat two-dimensional. I hooked them up to the DQ-20s and the speakers finally came alive. I liked the sound pretty well and gave them a decent review, but they weren't as special as my memory of the DQ-10s. And Harry was right about the BEL amplifiers' imaging being like "like paper ships on a paper sea." So I sold them soon after to someone from Totem Speakers for what I paid.

---

[16] Carl Marchisotto went on to found Alon and Nola speakers.

Michael Kuller

Dahlquist DQ-20 Speakers

BEL 1001 Series III Amplifier

I called Art Noxon at Acoustic Sciences Corporation to help me analyze what was going on in my room with the bass standing wave. We decided I needed some of his bass Tube Traps. Art said he had made some big custom ones for a manufacturer to use at a recent Consumer Electronics Show and could sell me those. In *IAR*, Peter Moncrieff had raved about the ASC Tube Traps and discussed properly placing them and rotating them for best sound. So I bought 18 of the four- and five-foot-tall Tube Traps and they arrived on four pallets one day. I stacked them, put them in the corners and along the front wall and they seemed to really help distribute the bass throughout the room. I had a few Room Tunes which I used for the first reflection points. There are Room Tunes pads above the curtains in front and on the first reflection points on the ceiling. The three Argent Room Lenses (resonator tubes) seemed to improve the imaging.

I was sent a pair of Counterpoint Clearfield Metropolitan speakers. I knew of Counterpoint because I had used one of their SA-2 tubed head amps before I bought a Vendetta head amp from John Curl, the best one I had heard.

The Metropolitan speakers were designed by Albert Von Schweikert who had designed the Vortex Screen speakers which garnered favorable reviews, in a venture with Counterpoint. Albert called and asked me if he could stop by my house and make some changes to the crossovers in the speakers. I told him to come on by. He arrived close to dinner time and I led him into the music room and he set to work on the speakers. Meanwhile, my wife and I and our girls sat down for dinner. I felt sorry for him sweating there working hard while we were having a nice family meal. After a couple of hours, he was finished, and I have to admit the speakers did sound better and were very nice sounding speakers.

Counterpoint Clearfield
Metropolitan Speakers

I reviewed or commented on a review of a pair of floor-standing ProAc speakers. They were very easy to drive and had a terrific midbass to upper midrange, so I sold the Thiel 3.5s and bought a pair of ProAc 3.5s. I had decided that using speakers with a bass equalizer probably wasn't the best for reviewing audio equipment. Eventually, I decided the ProAcs didn't have enough bass to satisfy me.

Proac Response 3.5 Speakers

In 1991 after Steve Winwood released his *Back in the High Life* album, since we liked it so much, we saw him two nights back to back at two different venues, Shoreline in Mountain View and the Concord Pavilion. At both concerts, the show started with a dark stage. Gradually we could hear the soft piano intro to "Low Spark of High Heeled Boys" as the lights came up slowly and we saw Winwood sitting at a grand piano. Terrific shows.

Steve Winwood
Photo by John Carrico

Michael Kuller

Chapter Six
The 90s

Consumer Electronic Shows

In the early and mid-1990s, I went to the Consumer Electronics Show in Las Vegas a few times. HP never went but would send one or two writers to cover the show and the rest of us could go, but we were on our own, expense-wise.

At my first Consumer Electronics Show, I met David Manley of Manley Labs and VTL with his son Luke. *Stereophile* had recently written a rave review of their VTL 300 amplifiers. I chatted with them for a short while and David insisted he wanted to send me a pair of his big Reference 600 (or 750) amplifiers. Whoa, I didn't need amplifiers that big. So we agreed on the Reference 350s. I liked them a lot so I ended up buying the pair and used them in my system and for comparisons. In 1993, VTL split off into a separate company run by Luke Manley. Then in 1996, David went back to Europe to work on products for studio recording that he had started out with. His younger fifth wife, EveAnna, took over Manley Labs and still runs it. She is a fun character and has done great things with the company and their equipment.

David Manley

EveAnna Manley

At Consumer Electronics Shows, I remember meeting Jonathan Scull, Jack English, Fred Kaplan, David Chesky, Myles Astor, Robert Harley, John Atkinson and even seeing J. Gordon Holt, plus all the high-end audio manufacturers and designers. Some experiences that stand out from those days at the Sahara were dinner with Bill Conrad and Lew Johnson, meeting Scot Markwell who was handling the equipment procurement for *TAS*, dinner with a number of *TAS* reviewers (including Michael Gindi and cable designer Roger Skoff), the porn stars being accompanied by bodyguards as they were paraded past the coffee shop up the escalators up to the X-Rated film exhibits, the *Stereophile* parties, seeing the Beach Boys perform with dancers in bikinis at a show, and just the great camaraderie between all the manufacturers, buyers and reviewers. It was fun, too, to hear the latest equipment and to find some new music.

At one Consumer Electronics Show, I met Mark Schifter of Audio Alchemy, a new digital products company. He sent me a couple of his products, including one to reduce jitter, a digital distortion. I tried them out and really liked them, so I bought them. Then I was recommended a new 75 ohm digital cable from Chris Sommovigo's company, Illuminati. I called him and bought one. My digital system continued to improve. Finally, in 1998, I dumped my separate CD transport, jitter reducer, and digital-to-analogue converter and bought a Wadia 850 all-in-one CD player with digital volume control. It was a big step up in sound quality.

At another Consumer Electronics Show, I saw Corey Green-berg, the popular, young gonzo writer for *Stereophile* (1990–1994). He was dressed in cowboy boots, jeans and a sport coat and was treated like a rockstar. A few years later he left the magazine and eventually became the Today Show's Tech Gadget Guru, hawking products he liked on the air. Then he was found to be taking kickbacks from the manufacturers, whose products he was promoting, and fired.

Corey Greenberg

Anecdotes

In 1995, Eugene Pitts, who had been the editor of *Audio Magazine* for 25 years, took over *The Audiophile Voice,* the publication from the Westchester Audio Society in New York and turned it into a smaller-sized national magazine. He published it for many years, and I used to find it on the local newsstands. I spoke to him on the telephone once, and he told me all he needed was 5,000 subscribers to keep it going. He also said he always featured musicians on the cover instead of audio equipment he was reviewing to give it a broader appeal.

It was 1995 when we went to see Bonnie Raitt perform at the Paramount Theater in Oakland. At the beginning of the concert, she announced they were recording the concert for a live album. She had a number of people join her onstage like Charles Brown, Ruth Brown, Bryan Adams, Kim Wilson and Jackson Browne. It was a terrific concert and the record was released in 1996 as her *Road Tested* double album.

Reviewing audio equipment is not as easy as it may look. You have to listen both critically, analyzing the different aspects of the sound, and in a relaxed state, noticing your emotional response to the music. Then there are the things you aren't aware of that can bubble up from your subconscious. I often had revelations about the sound or how to describe things when I was in the shower. Once you've nailed down equipment's sound, you have to write a very creative, interesting article about it, describing what you heard. *TAS* had some excellent writers, one had won a Pulitzer Prize and another had written a prize-winning series of detective novels. Reviewing for *TAS,* I didn't get much fan mail or letters about my reviews like some of the other writers, but HP said no one ever wrote to the magazine complaining that something I reviewed didn't sound as I described it. Most of my reviews were printed pretty much as I submitted them, with a few notes for revision, but

Michael Kuller

nothing major for the most part. My goal was to get the most out of the equipment I was working with to make it sound its best. After all, a bad review could really hurt a small manufacturer's business. People have criticized the magazine for not publishing more bad reviews, but if I couldn't get a component to sound good, I wouldn't want to spend all the hours necessary to listen and write about it. I'm sure the other writers felt the same way. And why would I want to write something positive about a product that didn't sound very good? After all, my reputation is all I had to create credibility for what I wrote—I wouldn't want to compromise it. Actually even positive reviews are critical about some aspects of the component's music reproduction.

In the mid-90s I was sent a pair of Wilson Audio WITTs, a three-way speaker in a single enclosure. Someone from Wilson came by to set them up and walked all around the room's walls banging two pieces of wood together to listen for slap echoes and find the best placement. He ended up placing them much farther back in the room and farther apart than I would normally put speakers. They didn't sound very good. I moved them all around and couldn't get them to sound any better. The midrange of the speaker seemed recessed with the highs and lows being forward. I eventually told the magazine I didn't like them and didn't want to review them, so I had them shipped back to Wilson. At the end of the year, the magazine asked the writers to list the best equipment they had listened to that year for The Product of the Year Awards. Always the iconoclast, I listed the WITT as the most disappointing product of the year for me. Later on, they were modified to a Series II and a couple of years later, dropped from the line.

Wilson WITT Speakers

I found that most speakers sound different with different amplifiers, so I wanted to try at least two different amplifiers with any speaker I reviewed. I recall trying three different amplifiers on a pair of speakers I was reviewing (the Thiel CS7s). Only one of the amplifiers clicked with them. Fortunately, I had one on hand. The same was true of amplifiers—I needed to have two different speakers to use them with. To compare two audio components, I found it is necessary to match the volumes of each carefully, with a 1,000 Hz tone and a digital multimeter.

Michael Kuller

Then over time, switching back and forth, I could hear more of the smaller differences between them and identify the gestalt of the component's sound. I found that matching a speaker to an amplifier is the most important combination after cartridge and tonearm matching.

In 1995, another magazine called *Fi* was started by businessman Larry Alan Kay in the Bay Area. Jonathan Valin and Wayne Garcia left *TAS* and were instrumental in starting it with a few other *TAS* writers joining them. I was told HP called Valin and Garcia "personas non gratis," saying they would never be welcome back at *TAS,* since he felt like they had stabbed him in the back.

Also in 1995, we took our daughters, five and nine years old, to their first concert to see the Beach Boys. This was the Cousin Mike Love/Bruce Johnston version. They were dancing in the aisles with everybody else to the songs they had heard many times at home. I always felt the girls' cultural education was important, so they grew up hearing the Beatles, Rolling Stones, Beach Boys, Motown and other classics I liked. One of my daughter's favorite movies in middle school was "Help!"

In 1996, I saw Ray Davies of the Kinks in a very memorable concert/performance. It was in San Francisco's tiny 500-seat Alcazar Theater. Davies read passages from his autobiography, *X-Ray,* he had just released. Accompanied by a second guitarist, he sang many of the Kinks' hit songs. Had it not been for a labor-union dispute in New York on their first US tour, opening for the Beatles, I think the Kinks would have been able to come back to tour the US again and would have been much bigger here.

I was sent a pair of Thiel CS7.0 speakers to review. I loved what they did and wrote a glowing review. After I sent it in, HP called me and said he thought they were a significant new loudspeaker and he had decided he wanted to write the main review. I argued that he had already assigned it to me, I put in a lot of work and had written a long review. So he followed my review with his review. The speakers worked best with my Manley Reference 350s, rather than either of the two solid-state amps I had on hand. I ended up buying the speakers and selling my ProAcs. They weighed 200lb each with their large molded concrete front baffles (to minimize cabinet vibrations which would affect the mid- and upper frequencies). They had a concentric tweeter/midrange driver and bass that extended very low in my room. They were also time and phase coherent with their first-order crossovers and sounded great. However, they were difficult to drive and needed a lot of power.

Get a Job

In 1998, I had just sold my second home-healthcare company and decided to take a year off to decide what to do next. I knew *TAS* was in financial difficulties, bankrupt for at least the second time, and I knew HP wanted to sell it to an investor to allow him to keep it going. He was never good at, or really interested in, the business part so he always turned that over to someone else. He didn't always choose the most trustworthy friends to do it. Plus, he was a pretty big spender. So I called HP and talked about buying the magazine and for a few minutes even considered the possibility. Me managing the magazine and HP? He sent me the paperwork and some financials, which I forwarded on to my business advisor/attorney. He said, "Are you crazy? What do you know about the publishing industry?" He was right, so I forgot about the fantasy of owning *TAS.*

I investigated a couple of other job opportunities and then the thought occurred to me—why not open a stereo store? Home theater was just beginning to take off, so I could have a video room in the store, too, and do home installations. With my background, I figured I have a lot of audio knowledge and know the brands I'd want to carry. I began to write a business plan as I looked around town and found a nice vacant location. I spoke to the landlord and he said he wanted to see my business plan first. I went back to work on it and started working on the financial pro forma. In the meantime, I talked to a number of people in the industry, two who had retail stores and a distributor. They all told me I must be nuts to try open a store now. Then as I finished the financial statement, I found that if the store didn't do well, it could cost me a whole lot of money. And if it did very well, I would make a salary I could probably live on. But the business would have little or no resale value because of the ease of entry into the business. If I could open one, so could someone else down the street. It would be extremely risky. I gave up the idea. And it's a good thing because after the home theater wave, the internet and mail order sadly replaced most of the brick-and-mortar audio stores. I ended up going back into home healthcare.

Audio Debates

There were always big debates in audio, and they got even bigger as the internet audio newsgroups started popping up. The biggest debate was between the subjectivists and the objectivists. The subjectivists believed, like HP, that your trained ears are much more sensitive to the sound of music reproduced through audio equipment than any steady-state measurements or tests. HP didn't like the term "subjective." He said what we did was "observational listening," just describing what we observed. (I figured it would be "subjective" if we said we liked the way the device sounded or discussed the sound in terms of our personal listening biases.) The objectivists believed that bench measurements and double-blind listening tests were necessary to determine if there were even audible differences between devices and to eliminate confirmation bias, where you would rate the more expensive or prettier component as better. Come on, we were paid professionals.

Then there were the tubed-versus-solid-state arguments. The tube guys said theirs sounded more realistic playing music because they reproduced the instruments' harmonic envelopes more completely and clipped much more softly when pushed. They said solid state sounded too analytical with its faster transients, grain and much less instrumental decay. The solid-state guys said their equipment was much more accurate with measurements and that the tube guys just liked hearing second harmonic distortion. This gap is closing—my new Rogue RP-7 tubed preamp sounds very neutral, not too soft or warm at all. If I didn't know, I wouldn't recognize the sound as coming from tubes.

There were also digital-versus-analogue debates. Analogue LPs sound more relaxed, warm and naturally musical they said. CDs sound edgy, artificial and not as realistic. The digital camp said their CDs didn't have noise, pops and clicks in the background. They were both right. Also, as time went on, digital (recordings and especially the playback equipment) got better and closed the gap. The first digitally recorded LP by a major label was Ry Cooder's, *Bop Till You Drop,* released in 1979. In the years and decades that followed, many LPs were recorded from digital tapes. Recently, everyone was surprised to find out that Mobile Fidelity Sound Labs, who remasters many recordings to sound better and gets great reviews from analogue purists, was using a digital step in their process, which they neglected to mention. The analogue lovers were shocked and some threatened a lawsuit. Now the analog purists are reviving reel-to-reel tapes.

I also found that long-term listening—hours over days and weeks—was necessary to reliably identify many of the more subtle audible differences between components and to determine whether they were an improvement to the reproduced music or not. Our brain is wired to notice differences, but deciding whether they are positive or negative is much harder. With quicker A/B listening, you can usually only identify large differences, like frequency response and noise. Besides long-term listening, I found that whether you looked forward to listening to a new component or not is important. If you do, it is probably doing something special to the music.

More Anecdotes

My wife's older brother, a couple of years younger than I am, is an artist and lived in the South of France for about 30 years. First he lived in a small studio apartment in Villefranche-Sur-Mer, just east of Nice. Then he got married and moved into a two-bedroom apartment across the small Mediterranean bay to St. Jean Cap Ferrat. This painting was one he did looking out his window toward Villefranche. I saw it at his place and bought it from him because I thought it captured the essence of the area. He had mentioned something about the Rolling Stones renting that house in the picture at one time. It wasn't until many years later when I read Keith Richard's excellent book, "Life," that I realized it's a painting of Villa Nellcôte, where the Rolling Stones had recorded *Exile on Main Street* in 1971.

The Thiel CS7.0 speakers were eventually upgraded to 7.2s. I ordered an upgrade kit and a buddy and I spent an afternoon swapping out all of the drivers, crossovers and components, everything except for the cabinets. Once broken in, the newer models seemed to do everything a little better and, with a simpler crossover, were easier to drive. They created a wide, deep soundstage with focused images and accurate timbre. They had wide dynamic contrasts and were very exciting.

In the late 1990s, I got a call from Scot Markwell that the magazine wanted me to review a pair of Merlin Speakers. Merlin owner, Bobby Palkovic, had a couple of manufacturers send me equipment to use with them. I got three complete sets of different level cables from Cardas. I also got a Joule Electra preamplifier and two Joule VZN-100MkII tubed amplifiers. But I never got the Merlins. Bobby Palkovic was known as being somewhat pushy and controlling, so I had heard. He called HP about his speaker review so many times that HP got fed up and cancelled the review. He went further and banned Bobby and Merlin from the magazine, even advertising in it. That was too bad, because I had heard a lot of good things about the two-way speaker. But the extra equipment came in handy.

Soon after this, the last full review I did was of Brian Cheney's 6 ft. tall VMPS FF-1 SRE Ribbon Speakers. How ironic. Brian really liked my newer listening room and I never mentioned the old *Stereophile* article. The speakers started off sounding terrible just hooked up to my system. I even asked Scot Markwell if I could get out of reviewing them, but he said he heard them at the Consumer Electronics Show and said they had sounded terrific, so he knew they had a lot of potential and encouraged me to keep working with them. We started playing around with equipment and cables, and finally got them sounding amazing, with some of the best sound in my room. This just shows the importance of good equipment matching. They were biamped with the Joule Electra amps for the ribbon (Cheney had used the same tweeky amps at the Consumer Electronics Show to demo the speakers), a Carver Sunfire amp for the bass and Cheney's electronic John Curl-designed crossover. Plus we substituted different speaker cables for the Transparent cables I was using. Cheney even sent Clark Johnsen (author of the *Wood Effect—Absolute Polarity Matters*) over one afternoon to hear them and listen with me. I remember putting on a Patricia Barber cut and remarking how seamless it sounded. Clark said that was due to the ribbon driver handling all of the midrange and high frequencies so there was nothing out of polarity or phase. But of course.

VMPS FF-1 SRE Ribbon Speaker

In 2000, *The Absolute Sound* magazine was finally purchased by businessman Tom Martin, and Valin and Garcia were brought back along with Robert Harley as editor. HP was pushed aside, given a small column, and I can't imagine how difficult it must have been for him to see his baby taken over and changed in front of his eyes. After 16 years with the magazine, I decided it was time for me to retire from listening to different audio equipment and to just enjoy listening to music for a change, so I bought a final system and left the magazine.

What I learned from over 40 years as an audiophile and 16 years of reviewing equipment is that tube–solid-state and analog–digital disagreements mostly come down to which distortions you can live with. Since there is no perfect sound, they all subtly distort the sound of the music that gets to our brain through our ears in one way or another. Some prefer solid-state distortions, while others prefer tubed, analog or digital distortions. System matching and synergy are about compensating for the distortions of each to create a sound that is more like real music to you. I found I needed to have tubes somewhere in my system. Since I listen to digital, I put together a final system designed to make CDs sound their best and loved listening to it for 20 years. It is shown in the pictures of my room on page 85.

Today, *Stereophile* and *The Absolute Sound* are still successful, regularly published and can be found on many newsstands. Most of the newer audio review publications today are online. Unfortunately, just about anyone can be an online audio-equipment reviewer, so you have to choose carefully. Enjoy the Music and Positive Feedback are a couple of the oldest and best. *Copper Magazine,* published by PS Audio and edited by Frank Doris, is also very interesting. The Daily Audiophile.com lists about 100 online audio publications with links to their sites.

Epilogue
And the Beat Goes On

We continued to see some great live music. In 2001, we went to the JVC Jazz Festival at the Concord Pavilion and saw Diana Krall singing with her piano and combo backed by a symphony orchestra. I still use her song "I've Got You Under My Skin" from her album with an orchestra, *When I Look into Your Eyes,* as a reference.

Diana Krall
Photo by Bonnie Perkinson

In 2005, I took my 15-year-old daughter, who loves music, to see the Rolling Stones at a big stadium and bought 14th row tickets so she could see them up close. She loved it, especially seeing them do "Sympathy for the Devil" with Mick up at the top of the scaffolding over the stage wearing a top hat.

That same year, I took my daughter with us to see Steve Winwood at a small outdoor venue. When he played "Gimme Some Lovin'," I told her that the song was 45 years old. I asked her if she thought any of the new music she was listening to would be around that long, or even 20 years from now. She said, "I really doubt it." And now, nearly 20 years later, a few of her groups are still around, like Death Cab, Panic at the Disco and Franz Ferdinand.

That year, my daughter handed me a Foo Fighters double album called *In Your Honor* she had bought. She said, "Here, Dad, I think you'll like the second CD." The first CD was harder rock and the second was mellower acoustic rock. I really liked that one. The next year, the Foo Fighters came to town to do a mostly acoustic concert, so I bought tickets and took her. We had a great time. It was a musical memory to cherish.

When my younger daughter left for college, we downsized and moved to the next town to a tract house with a nice, smaller living room I could use for my music and my audio system. I had carpet installed over the hardwood floor, added inexpensive curtains, three dedicated 20-amp circuits and hospital-grade electrical outlets plus French doors with double pane glass for soundproofing. It took me about five months to get the system to sound like I wanted. I positioned the speakers first, then moved all of the Tube Traps in and out one at time, then a few at a time to assess the sound. I ended up using all of them. The small 14' X 17' X 8' room shouldn't have sounded as good with the big Thiels and all the Tube Traps, but it did. With all the sound treatment, I figured we pretty much eliminated the sound of the room entirely, which seemed to work. The stage the system produced was wide and deep with great 3D imaging. A musician friend who makes CDs of his band's music said it sounded like he was in the studio listening to the monitors. I took that as a big compliment. We lived here for 12 years. I found myself listening with friends who were music lovers instead of audiophiles. I would invite a few of them over from time to time for "rock and roll night," drinking red wine, having a couple of puffs and playing some great music. I have friends who are both a little older and younger than I am so it's interesting how their musical tastes differ from mine, focusing on older or newer music depending mostly on their ages. Fortunately, there's a lot of overlap. It appears our musical tastes are formed during our high school and college years. I'm just glad mine coalesced when it did.

In 2008, I moved to a smaller house and turned the 17' X 14' X 8' living room into my dedicated listening room by adding carpet, three dedicated 20-amp electrical circuits and French doors. Left rear view.

Michael Kuller

Right front view showing equipment and Salamander rack. CD player is a Wadia 850 connected directly to Manley Neo-Classic amps. Cables are impedance-matched MIT Oracle V3s and speakers are Thiel 7.2s.

Right rear view with CD rack. Listening spot on the couch is 34" from the back wall. I experimented with the sound treatment from my old room and ended up preferring it all placed in here.

This is the view from my listening spot. The speaker fronts are 3' 8" from the front wall and 2' 10" on center from the side walls. They are 8' 6" apart. (My daughter gave me the lava lamp for Xmas.)

The listening spot is 10' from the speakers. The sound in this room is less expansive and deep, but more immediate and intimate than in the previous room, which was two and a half times larger.

Michael Kuller

Left-front view of the room showing the inexpensive lined drapes from Penny's.

In 2009 we saw Joe Cocker open and then Steve Winwood together with Eric Clapton (my first time seeing him) in concert. My wife doesn't care for Joe Cocker but liked his performance that night (he passed away in 2014). The concert was excellent and there is a CD recorded from their tour—*Live from Madison Square Garden. Layla* and *Blind Faith* are two of my favorite albums, so this was one of my top five favorite concerts.

Winwood and Clapton

In the summer of 2010, we took our daughter with us to see Paul McCartney at a big stadium. He puts on a great show and she couldn't believe she was actually seeing a Beatle live. Me, too.

Sir Paul

Photo by Dave Lipton

Michael Kuller

Then, in 2012, we saw Roger Waters perform *The Wall* at Pac Bell Park from about the 20th row down on the field. When the helicopter came in at the beginning of "Another Brick in the Wall," it sounded so realistic that we found ourselves ducking and looking around behind us. There were some large speakers on high towers there for surround sound we hadn't noticed but no helicopter. The visual effects that covered the entire area in front of us were terrific. And the music was good, too, although Waters needed two different lead guitarists to take the place of David Gilmour.

The Wall
Photo by Jim Baikovicius

In 2015, we went to one of the biggest and best musical events I've been to—JazzFest in New Orleans. It goes on over two 3-day weekends, but we could only make the second one. We got in on a Thursday and saw Saint Paul and the Broken Bones at Tipitina's Club that night. The next two days, we spent at JazzFest seeing headliners like Jerry Lee Lewis, Chicago and Elton John. We also saw other terrific zydeco, rock, blues, brass bands, creole, Dixieland and straight jazz on smaller stages all over the place. Second Line parades came through from time to time decked out in their traditional garb. Unfortunately, we missed The Who perform on the previous weekend and Steve Winwood's performance on the Sunday we left. It was still phenomenal; I recommend everyone who loves music go there at least once. There's nothing like it.

Jazzfest

Also in 2015, we went to see The Moody Blues for the first time. Graeme Edge, at 74, was still playing drums (he had a stroke the next year) and there was a second drummer on the other side of the stage playing along with him. Ray Thomas played flute (he passed away in 2018). John Lodge, at 70 on bass, strutted around the stage with his shirt open like a young rock star. And Justin Hayward still had one of the best voices in rock music. It was a terrific concert.

After 20 years of listening to "my final system," we decided to downsize again to a condominium in 2021. I put an ad on AudioGon to sell my entire system with the room treatments, CDs (since I had all the music on my iTunes in Lossless) and everything else audio for a single price of $12,500, hoping to

Michael Kuller

sell it locally. That seemed like a long shot, but it looked like the easiest way to sell it all since I didn't want to have to ship my 200lb speakers or all the Tube Traps. And this was in late 2020 during COVID. A couple of people contacted me who were interested in buying my amplifiers and even one local guy was interested in my speakers. Then a guy contacted me and said he was interested in buying everything, but he was on vacation and couldn't come over to see it for a week. So I waited. He was the first to come over, was in his late 30s, lived nearby in a very exclusive area and was a serious audiophile. He said he worked making a special computer for use in race cars that he had invented. He sat down, listened to a couple of songs and just like that, said he'd take the entire system. He reached into the pocket of his sweatpants and took out the full price I had listed it for, in cash, and handed it to me. He said his neighbor had a moving company and arranged a day for him to come pick it all up. Then it was all gone. That really was a pleasant surprise. Was that good luck or what?

Once in the condominium (two bedrooms, den, 1550sq ft, single level upstairs, about the size of our first house), I had the challenge of putting a new system together that would also provide sound for the TV in the much smaller space. Fortunately, in the condo we liked the best, the previous owner had the fireplace removed, so there was a good place to locate the stereo system. I went to San Francisco and listened to three pair of speakers that seemed to have potential from the reviews I had read: the new Paradigm 80Fs (driven by a less expensive Luxman integrated), the Golden Ear Triton 2+s and the Vandersteen Treo CTs. The Vandys sounded the best to me by far. Driven by a tubed McIntosh amp, they did a terrific job on the instruments and especially the drums of Dave Brubeck's "Take Five."

I started out with a Parasound HINT6 integrated, but found it inadequate. I'm now using a used Parasound Halo A21+ amplifier, designed by John Curl, and a new Rogue RP-7 tubed preamplifier, which seems to be about the best tubed model on the market now for the money. For a streamer/music storage I'm using a Bluesound Vault 2i. I wasn't satisfied with their DAC, so I added a better one, a Chord Qutest. It made a big improvement.

But the sound with my digital music and solid-state amp still had a little glare in the upper midrange I needed to warm up. I talked to the two tube gurus, Brent at Brentjessee and Andy at Vintage Tube Services for suggestions. I tried four different pair of input tubes in the Rogue, and Andy's suggestion of NOS Mullard shortplates were the best. He said I was the second person that week to order them for an RP-7.

Michael Kuller

I also have a Bluesound Powernode 2i for my NHT outdoor speakers on the deck. Cabling and power conditioning are all from AudioQuest.[17] Now I have no physical media for music plus I can control everything on my phone or laptop from the couch. It's the ultimate in audiophile convenience. For room treatment, I put a decorative 4' X 6' rug on the back wall and I can let down the shades over the windows and sliding door. This is a real compromise without having a dedicated room and better room treatments. The stage is not as expansive or deep, but the instruments and vocals are separated clearly, sound realistic and are satisfying.

My daughter is in her 30s now and still loves music, but she hasn't become an audiophile. I've passed on my A/V receivers and speakers to her as I've upgraded over the years. She went down to Magnolia at Best Buy and checked out the headphones on their comparison rack. She picked out a $250 pair of Audio Technicas she liked best. She's collecting LPs; for Christmas last year, I gave her a Pro-Ject Basic turntable. Her musical tastes are much more eclectic than mine—she listens to a very wide variety of artists in different genres on Spotify.

---

[17] Thanks to Shane Buettner for his advice.

My near lifelong musical–audio journey has come to a good resting spot for now. There are still musical performances I want to see, but fewer and fewer as the great acts get older, stop performing or fade away. Now we are happy to go see good cover bands of the Beatles, Tom Petty and Pink Floyd. I never get tired of listening to my classic music, or "oldies" as my daughter calls them. But what a time to have grown up.

I was born at the right time to witness the growth of popular music from the 1950s with Elvis and rhythm and blues to the 1960s/1970s classic rock and psychedelia. Then to the 1980s disco and the pop music of the next few decades. It's the greatest music ever made. How many people have had an opportunity to see all the artists I've seen in their prime and enjoy the excitement of the artist's recordings as they were released?

In audio, I was there for the birth of high-end audio equipment and the underground audio review publications that wrote about them. It was great fun and an amazing experience to be in the middle of that. I had some great audio equipment and systems. I was able to meet some great people in the industry and to listen to even more of the great audio equipment being produced. Finally, I was fortunate enough to have written for the top publication in the industry for 16 years in its prime. I was a very lucky guy.

As pharmacist/entrepreneur, I was again in the right place at the right time to get in on the home healthcare boom of the mid-1980s and 1990s.

Yes, what a great time to have been born, to have lived and to be alive! Lucky me, to have been an outlier.

Michael Kuller

Appendices

Appendix I—Concert List

In the 1990s, I started saving ticket stubs and making this list.

Year	Band	Venue
1965	Pyramids	Roswell Armory
	We Five/Righteous Brothers	ENMU Gym
1967	Doors	Family Dog – Denver
1968	Jimi Hendrix	Regis College Field House
	Four Tops	Fontainebleau Hotel – Miami
	Janis Joplin/Steve Miller	Denver Arena
1969	David Essex/BB King/Rolling Stones	Colo. State Gym
	Santana/CSN	Denver Arena
1970	Blues Image/Mountain	CU Practice Field
1971	John Kay/Black Sabbath	Denver Arena
	The Who (*Who's Next*)	Denver Arena
	Rod Stewart and the Faces	Denver Arena
	Yes/Allman Brothers	Denver Arena
	Mountain	CU Practice Field
	James Gang	Denver Arena
	Long John Baldry / Savoy Brown / Fleetwood Mac	CU Field house
	West, Bruce and Laing	CU Field House
1972	James Gang	Denver Arena
	Joe Walsh Barnstorm	Tulagi Club
	Bonnie Raitt	Denver Arena
	War	Tulagi Club
	Vanilla Fudge / Ten Years After	Red Rocks
	Hugh Masekela / Woody Herman	Red Rocks
	Mountain	Red Rocks
1973	Randy Newman	Ebbets Field Club
	Leon Russell	Denver Club
	Captain Beefheart	Ebbets Field Club
	Ramsey Lewis	Denver Bar/Club
	Eddie Harris	Denver Jazz Club
1973–78	Linda Ronstadt/Eagles (*On the Border*)	Santa Monica Civic
	Bonnie Raitt / Jackson Browne	Santa Monica Civic
	Montrose / Firesign Theater	Santa Monica Civic
	Led Zeppelin	Long Beach Arena
	Joan Baez	Hollywood Bowl
	Leon Redbone / The Band	Greek Theater LA
	Steve Martin / Linda Ronstadt	Universal Amphitheater
	Jackson Browne X 2	Universal Amphitheater
	Loggins and Messina	Universal Amphitheater
	Linda Ronstadt X 2	Universal Amphitheater
	Seals and Croft	Universal Amphitheater

Year	Band	Venue
	Fleetwood Mac	Universal Amphitheater
	Tom Scott / Joni Mitchell	Universal Amphitheater
	Manhattan Transfer	Roxy Club LA
	Heart / Foreigner / Eagles / Steve Miller	Oakland Coliseum (Day on the Green)
	Dave Mason	Universal Amphitheater
	Little Feat	Berkeley Community Theater
1979	Captain Beefheart	Boarding House in SF
	Boz Scaggs	Greek Theater Berkeley
1980	Randy Newman / Bonnie Raitt	Greek Theater
1981	Peter Allen	Nicasio Inn
	Bonnie Raitt, Bill Payne, Paul Barrere	Great American Music Hall
	Tubes	Old Waldorf SF
1982	Paul Simon (*Graceland*)	Berkeley Community Theater
	Georgie Fame / Van Morrison	Berkeley Community Theater
	Yes (*90125*)	Greek Theater
	Dire Straits	Concord Pavilion
	Pat Metheny	Greek Theater
	Howard Jones / Eurythmics	Greek Theater
	Brian Ferry	Greek Theater
	Police	Greek Theater
	Mitch Woods / Stevie Ray Vaughan	Keystone Berkeley
	Heart	Concord Pavilion
	Jackson Browne	Oakland Arena
	Blues Brothers	Concord Pavilion
	James Taylor	Concord Pavilion
	Kenny Loggins	Greek Theater
	Huey Lewis and the News	Greek Theater
1983	Beach Boys	Napa County Fair
	Joan Armatrading	Greek Theater
1984	Pretenders	Bill Graham Civic
1985	Stan Getz (*Dolphin*)	Keystone SF
	Art Blakey and the Jazz Messengers	Keystone SF
	S.F. Symphony X 3	Davies Hall
	Stevie Ray Vaughan	Greek Theater
	Rory Block	Larry Blake's Berkeley
	Bruce Springsteen	Oakland Coliseum
	Rickie Lee Jones	Warfield SF
1986–88	SF Symphony – 2 yrs, 8 shows each	Davies Hall
	Art Blakey and the Jazz Messengers	Keystone SF
	Amanda McBroom	Bimbo's SF
1988	George Thorogood / Allman Brothers	Concord Pavilion
1989	Don Henley	Concord Pavilion
1990	Stevie Ray Vaughan	Concord Pavilion
	Heart	Concord Pavilion
	Robert Cray	Berkeley Community Theater

Year	Band	Venue
1991	Sting (with Branford Marsalis)	Concord Pavilion
	Steve Winwood X 2	Shoreline & Concord Pav.
	Don Henley	Concord Pavilion
1992	Chris Isaac / Santana	Concord Pavilion
	Diablo Symphony	Lesher Center
1993	Lyle Lovett	Greek Theater
	Tina Turner	Concord Pavilion
	Robben Ford	Slim's SF
1994	Bridge Benefit – Neil Young, Tom Petty	Shoreline
	Traffic (Reunion)	Concord Pavilion
1995	Boz Scaggs	Greek Theater
	Beach Boys	Concord Pavilion
	Hootie and the Blowfish	Greek Theater
	Bonnie Raitt	Paramount Theater
1996	Ray Davies	Alcazar Theater SF
	Lyle Lovett	Greek Theater
	Shawn Colvin / Jackson Browne	Greek Theater
1997	Tom Petty	Fillmore
	Boz Scaggs	Fillmore
	Rolling Stones	Oakland Coliseum
1998	Smokey Robinson	Wente
1999	Boz Scaggs	Wente
	Steve Winwood	Mountain Winery
2000	Steely Dan	Concord Pavilion
	K.D.Lang / Sting	Concord Pavilion
	Beach Boys	Concord Pavilion
2001	Diana Krall (JVC JazzFest)	Concord Pavilion
	James Taylor	Concord Pavilion
	Patricia Barber	Yoshi's Oakland
2002	Bonnie Raitt	Paramount Theater
	Jackson Browne / Tom Petty	Greek Theater
2003	Jackson Browne	Greek Theater
	Robben Ford	Yoshi's
	Dick Dale	Slim's SF
	Dave Mason	Slim's SF
	Simon and Garfunkel (Reunion)	Oakland Arena
2004	Yes (Reunion)	Concord Pavilion
	Keb' Mo' / Bonnie Raitt	Greek Theater
	Lee Ritenour	Yoshi's
	Doobie Brothers	Fillmore
	James Taylor	Concord Pavilion
	Indigenous	Slim's SF
	Black Crowes / Tom Petty	Greek Theater
	Rolling Stones	Pac Bell Park

Michael Kuller

Year	Band	Venue
2005	Diana Krall	Yoshi's
	Loggins and Messina (Reunion)	Greek Theater
	Steve Winwood	Wente
2006	Foo Fighters (Acoustic tour)	Fox Theater
	Chicago / Earth, Wind and Fire	Greek Theater
	Tom Petty	Greek Theater
2007	Police (Reunion)	Oakland Coliseum
	Steve Winwood	Fillmore
	Robben Ford	Yoshi's
	James Gang (Reunion)	Mountain Winery
	Brian Wilson (*Pet Sounds*)	Fox Theater
2008	Steely Dan	Greek Theater
	Steve Miller	Fillmore
	Los Lonely Boys	Fillmore
2009	Davey Knowles / Jeff Beck (Tal bass)	Fox Theater
	Chicago / Earth, Wind and Fire	Concord Pavilion
	Doobie Brothers	Fillmore
	Joe Cocker / Clapton – Winwood	Oakland Arena
	Lydia Pense and Cold Blood	Todos Santos Plaza Concord
	Willie Nelson	Fillmore
2010	Tommy Castro	Yoshi's
	Paul McCartney	Pac Bell Park
	Tom Petty	Oakland Arena
	Huey Lewis	Wente
	Los Lonely Boys	KFOG KaBoom Pier 32
2011	Buffalo Springfield (Reunion)	Fox Theater
	Sonny Landreth	Bankhead Theater
2012	Roger Waters (*The Wall*)	Pac Bell Park
	Mavis Staples / Bonnie Raitt	Greek Theater
2013	The Who (*Quadrophenia*)	Oakland Arena
	Pink	Sydney, Australia
	Michael McDonald / Boz Scaggs	Cache Creek
2014	Steve Winwood	Wente
	John Mayall	Lesher Audit
	Boz Scaggs	Fox Theater
2015	St. Paul and the Broken Bones	Tipitina's
	Elton John, Chicago, Jerry Lee Lewis	New Orleans JazzFest
	Moody Blues	Fox Theater
	David Lindley / Jackson Browne	Greek Theater
	Hall and Oates	Greek Theater
	Boz Scaggs	Fox Theater
	Cheap Trick / Peter Frampton	Wente
	Leon Russell	Yoshi's
	The Who	Oakland Arena

Year	Band	Venue
2016	Dave Mason	Uptown Napa
	Stevie Wonder, Buddy Guy, Ziggy Marley, Florence and the Machine	Bottlerock Napa
	Paul Simon	Greek Theater
	Robert Cray / Boz Scaggs	Wente
	Bad Co. / Lou Gramm (Foreigner)	Ironstone Amphitheater Murphys
	The Tubes	Santa Cruz boardwalk
	Bonnie Raitt	Fox Theater
2017	Doobie Bros / Chicago	Concord Pavilion
	Roger Waters	Oakland Arena
2018	Paul Simon	Oakland Arena
	Tommy Castro	Todos Santos Plaza
	Boz Scaggs	Chautauqua Theater Boulder
	Ventures	Cornerstone Berkeley
2019	Tower of Power	Fox Theater
	Temptations / Four Tops	Paramount Theater
	The Fixx	Santa Cruz boardwalk
2021	Jackson Browne	Oxbow Napa
	Meyer Hawthorne	Bimbo's SF
	Van Morrison	Oxbow Napa

Appendix II—MK's Listening Biases

Published in *The Absolute Sound* Issue 80, June 1992.

DESCRIBING my listening biases has always been somewhat difficult for me to do; they're a part of me I just take for granted, like recognizing my face when I look in the mirror. But ask me to describe what I look like and... well, I have two eyes, a nose, thinning hair on top, uh... I think you know what I mean.

My musical tastes tend toward retro-Seventies rock, which means the artists and musical styles I listened to in college[1] that are now regaining popularity with a different generation, such as Steve Winwood, Little Feat, Bonnie Raitt, Jackson Browne, various blues artists, and the like. I find jazz relaxing and enjoy classical music from time to time, especially after hearing an inspiring performance by the San Francisco Symphony.

As to what I listen for, musically involving sound which draws me in to the performance is my first priority. Of course, I prefer tonal neutrality and lack of colorations, especially throughout the midrange, but if the sound errs to one side or the other, I would prefer that it be toward the warm and romantic, rather than the cold and analytical. Most of all, it must sound *believable*, as though it could be emanating from real people and instruments. Usually, that means that sounds can be masked, but no unnatural colorations should be added to make the sound unnatural. Errors of omission are preferred to those of commission. Next on my list: realistic dynamic contrasts that are the life and breath of the music, and a seamless coherence throughout the frequency range with no peaks or dips. In these two areas particularly, I believe we still have a long way to go toward re-creating the experience of live music.

The reproduction of a spacious and well-defined soundstage with three-dimensional images is more important to me than to many of my colleagues. It still astonishes me that stereo sound is capable of creating such a "visual" effect, which can bring me that much closer to the illusion of having the musicians there in the room with me. As my room becomes fine-tuned, I constantly am surprised at the improvements that can be achieved in these parameters.

Frequency extension at both extremes is important. Good bass is necessary for a solid foundation which connects to the emotions, and the high frequencies need to be present for a proper sense of delicacy and air. Live music is not bandwidth limited.

The Room

For the past 15 or so years that I have been involved in High End audio, I have always carefully considered the layout of the living room when renting or buying a house. Finding the perfect audio room was always high on the list of my priorities, although there always have been compromises. After purchasing a lot on which to build a house, I took the opportunity to design a room off to one side for use as a dedicated listening room. Enlisting the help of David Walsh from Walsh-Norris Designs, a San Francisco acoustic design firm, I discovered that there were two goals I should work toward. The first was to reduce the effect of standing waves in the lower frequencies by selecting good room dimensions. With a rectangular-shaped room, it's not possible to eliminate standing waves entirely, but their effect can be minimized. As much as possible, the ceiling height and wall lengths should not be multiples of the same number or of each other.

The second goal was to keep as much of the music in the room as possible. Ordinarily, the floor and walls can flex and absorb sound, particularly in the lower frequencies, and transmit the sound to adjacent rooms. Making the floor solid and the walls stiff and separated from the adjoining walls was very important. A third goal was to keep the cost within reason.

The room that resulted is relatively large, 17-feet wide by 27-feet long with a 10-1/2-foot coffered (or soffited, as some call it) ceiling. The front end of the room is shaped like a bay with large, double-paned windows in each section. This entire end of the room can be covered by floor to ceiling drapes to damp early reflections. The rear of the room has double french doors with thick, laminated glass. The floor is a solid concrete slab covered with carpet and a pad. The walls are double layers of 5/8-inch sheetrock attached to alternating offset studs on 20-inch centers. This decouples the other side of the wall, and the insulation in between helps keep the

---

[1] *Might I add that while in college I purchased a copy of* Casino Royale. *Little did I know that it was destined for collectible status, and that I would pay over 10 times the original price to own it again some years later.*

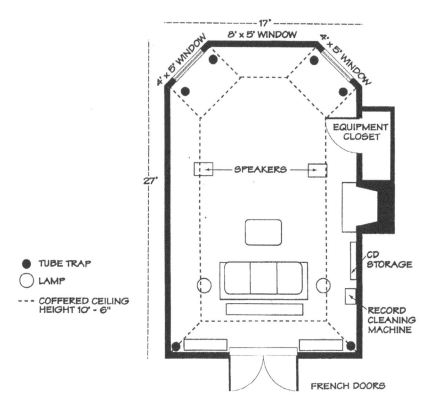

● TUBE TRAP

○ LAMP

--- COFFERED CEILING
    HEIGHT 10' - 6"

sound from transmitting to the next room, and keeps external noise from coming in. The ceiling is constructed of two layers of sheetrock separated by a resilient channel.

On one side of the room there is a walk-in equipment closet with ten hospital-grade outlets fed by five individual 20-amp circuits. The five non-adjustable built-in shelves, which are open in the rear for easy access, are made of oak an inch thick and designed to support over 100 pounds each.

From the first time I stepped into the finished room, it was obvious the acoustics were different here than in the other rooms of the house. Although the room was empty, there was little of the echo/reverberation of voices one would expect. When I spoke, my voice seemed much clearer and more articulate; I could more easily hear the sound of vocal cords in my throat and the air in my chest resonating.

Once the few pieces of furniture were moved in, my equipment was set up, and I began playing music, the sound immediately seemed more detailed from top to bottom than it had been in my previous listening rooms, with images more solidly anchored in space. Since then, I have experimented with

speaker placement in relation to my listening position and have added both ASC Tube Traps and RoomTunes. The Tube Traps have greatly improved the quality of the bass by removing some of the lower frequency standing waves (identified by using a CD with test tones[2]). Like TOM, I have found that RoomTunes are very useful in fine-tuning the room's acoustics. The CornerTunes and EchoTunes are surprisingly effective at improving soundstaging and smoothing out rough edges.

Having a room like this to experiment with and move equipment in and out of without regard to aesthetics has made me more aware of how important the listening environment is to sound quality. The room is truly the "final component," and small adjustments can make big differences, especially in the quality of soundstaging and imaging, and in the smoothness of frequency response. Fine-tuning the acoustics will be a long-term project and will most likely need to begin all over again, to a certain extent, each time I change loudspeakers.

—MK

---

[2] *Available from ASC (1-800-ASC-TUBE).*

Acknowledgements

I would like to thank Richard Colburn and Garrett Hongo for writing books about their audio experiences, which encouraged me to write about mine. I would also like to thank John Morris for his editing and formatting, Jon Hioki for the cover design, and John Atkinson for his suggestions.

Made in the USA
Las Vegas, NV
12 December 2023

82637964R00085